30 Minutes to Mealtime

Easy recipes for great-tasting meals ...from the Kitchens of General Foods

Introduction

Taking time to prepare a home-cooked meal can be a pleasure for those of us who enjoy cooking—*when* there's time to do it. However, even the most devoted cook often has a hungry family anxiously waiting for them to "bring on the food." Sound familiar? If so, this handy publication may soon become your favorite kitchen companion.

30 Minutes to Mealtime is designed to help ease your time crunch in the kitchen. We've tapped the culinary expertise of our special team of home economists from the General Foods Test Kitchens to develop this delightful volume of convenient recipes perfect for today's busy lifestyles. Each great-tasting recipe can be prepared easily in just 30 minutes . . . *or less.* You can't even get most pizzas delivered faster than that! Most importantly, you'll discover each recipe, showcasing great-tasting ingredients from the Kraft General Foods family of fine products, to be as satisfying as it is delicious!

*All recipes can be prepared in 30 minutes or less, after ingredients and cooking utensils are assembled.

NO TIME TO COOK? THINK AGAIN!

In the same amount of time it takes to pick up take-out or to eat out, battling traffic and long lines at fast-food restaurants, you can serve an appealing, satisfying and usually less expensive meal at home. It just takes a little preliminary planning.

GETTING ORGANIZED

Organization is one of the first steps in managing efficient meal preparation.

Kitchen Arrangement—Make sure foods, utensils and equipment are arranged conveniently for fast paced work.

Pantry Planning—Have the essentials on hand. Keep your cabinets, refrigerator and freezer stocked with quick-to-fix ingredients that can be used in a variety of ways for easy last minute meal preparation. You should have an assortment of fresh and frozen vegetables, chicken pieces and ground beef or turkey. Also, stock the pantry with handy mealtime helpers such as GOOD SEASONS Salad Dressing Mix,

LOG CABIN Syrup, MINUTE Rice, SHAKE 'N BAKE Seasoning and Coating Mix and STOVE TOP Stuffing Mix, to make meal planning effortless.

Keep GOOD SEASONS Salad Dressing Mixes on hand for quick sauces and easy marinades. Use STOVE TOP Stuffing Mix in the Canister to hurry up Monday's casserole or Thursday's skillet dish. Keep MINUTE Rice ready for one-dish suppers in a pinch. You'll be amazed how these products make quick work out of weekday meals. To save time in preparation, buy boneless chicken, pork or beef, or purchase store-cooked roast meats and poultry at the deli counter for recipes calling for cooked or leftover meat. In a pinch, use frozen chopped onions and peppers instead of chopping fresh ones.

Meal Ideas—Try to plan at least some meals in advance. This can be as simple as thinking about what you plan to serve for dinner tomorrow so any defrosting or last minute shopping is anticipated. When possible, map out a few meals and make a grocery list.

Shopping Lists—Keep a pad of paper attached to or near the refrigerator for jotting down items as you need them.

Know the Score—Read recipes ahead to be sure you have all ingredients on hand. Think about a logical order for tasks in preparing the meal. Then assemble the equipment and ingredients you need.

TIME-SAVING STRATEGIES

Do some preparation steps ahead—While dinner is cooking, use those free minutes to get a head start on tomorrow night's meal.

• Thaw frozen meat, fish or poultry overnight in the refrigerator.

• To make salads quickly, do the work in advance. Wash a few bunches of greens. Spin or pat dry and store in plastic bags in the refrigerator; they should keep for a few days.

• Prepare vegetables for cooking or salads the day before, or even earlier. Package in tightly sealed plastic bags before refrigerating.

• Use leftovers wisely. Leftovers from the Sunday roast chicken can make a wonderful casserole or stir-fry during the week. Saturday night chili becomes a great topper for Monday's taco salad or quick-cooked rice.

Use time-saving methods
• Take advantage of kitchen helpers—small appliances such as your food processor, chopper or blender. They make traditionally time-consuming tasks go faster.

• Quick cooking methods such as grilling, stir-frying and microwaving can cut cooking time.

Get others to pitch in—Have your children or spouse help with simple preparation steps, setting and clearing the table or washing dishes.

Work smart—When you *do* have time to cook, make your efforts pay off. On weekends, for example, make a double batch of stew, spaghetti sauce or soup for the freezer.

Good Food, Great Taste... Without The Wait!

The secret to simplifying weekday meal preparation is using recipes that start with great tasting, high quality ingredients you can pull from your shelf in a snap. With our helpful line of popular Kraft General Foods products, a home-cooked meal has never been easier! And, great taste is assured.

For over 40 years, MINUTE Rice has been America's favorite instant rice. And there's a good reason for that—MINUTE Rice starts with the finest quality long grain rice that cooks up light and fluffy—perfect every time! MINUTE Rice is also the foundation for many appetizing RICE-IPES—easy, wholesome, delicious recipes the whole family will enjoy, made in 30 minutes or less.

In this publication, we've included recipes using three MINUTE Rice varieties that are sure to please everyone—MINUTE Original Rice, MINUTE Premium Long Grain Rice and MINUTE Instant Brown Rice.

Fresh recipes start with GOOD SEASONS Salad Dressing Mix. You make it fresh . . . you make it best.® The dressing mixes contain a unique blend of herbs and spices—you add your own choice of oil and vinegar to assure fresh flavor. With GOOD SEASONS, creating the perfect complement for any salad is always easy.

Distinctively delicious GOOD SEASONS Salad Dressing Mixes give you a choice to meet your special needs—GOOD SEASONS Salad Dressing Mix, GOOD SEASONS Reduced Calorie Salad Dressing or GOOD SEASONS Nonfat Salad Dressing Mix. And they come in a wide variety of popular flavors. Whether it's the robust taste of Zesty Italian or the sweet and tangy taste of Honey Mustard, each unique GOOD SEASONS blend makes ordinary recipes absolutely mouth-watering.

Think of LOG CABIN Syrup, and you probably think of a tantalizing breakfast—stacks of pancakes swirled with syrup, maybe a little bacon and piping hot coffee.

First introduced in 1887, LOG CABIN is the oldest national brand of syrup on supermarket shelves. And now delicious LOG CABIN Syrup is available in regular and lower calorie versions to suit your special needs. Today LOG CABIN Syrup is not just for breakfast! In this publication, you'll find mouth-watering ways to use syrup in great tasting entrees, side dishes and desserts.

Stove Top®

For a delicious change of pace, treat the family to STOVE TOP Stuffing instead of potatoes! Whether in the box or convenient easy-to-use canister, STOVE TOP fits your style:

STOVE STOP Stuffing Mix in the Box—Specially baked stuffing crumbs that come with a special vegetable-seasoning packet. Ready in minutes, it makes a delicious side dish that's an exciting alternative to potatoes any night of the week.

STOVE TOP Stuffing Mix in the Canister—All the savory seasonings are in the pre-coated stuffing crumbs, so you can measure out and make exactly the amount you need. Versatility is built in, making the canister variety perfect for recipes.

All the STOVE TOP recipes in this publication use STOVE TOP Stuffing Mix in the Canister. Included are convenient and exciting one-dish stuffing suppers, easy entrees and splendid side dishes.

You can count on SHAKE 'N BAKE Seasoning and Coating Mixes to add special flavor and preserve the juicy taste of chicken, pork and fish *without frying*. SHAKE 'N BAKE is so easy to prepare, just moisten, shake and bake. That's it!

Since SHAKE 'N BAKE comes in an assortment of flavors, you can treat your family to something different each time you serve it. Original and Hot & Spicy varieties give your chicken or pork a crispy coating that keeps the meat juicy on the inside. Barbecue flavors create a moist glaze that makes meat taste like it's right off the grill! For added variety, you can also use an assortment of poultry pieces. SHAKE 'N BAKE is *great* on boneless skinless chicken breasts.

Creative Beginnings

Simple, yet delicious recipes—that's what busy cooks need when serving family or friends. Whether in search of a quick dip, fast finger food or satisfying soup, these recipes are for you — tempting Confetti Dip, Pita Crisps, Tangy Chicken Wings, Sausage-Stuffed Mushrooms, Hearty Minestrone and more.

Page through this chapter for delicate appetizers sure to satisfy the light snacker or substantial soups for those with a heartier appetite. Each tasty recipe makes something very special out of a handful of simple ingredients and a few short minutes in the kitchen. Many of these starters can even be enjoyed as light entrees as well.

Tangy Chicken Wings

- ½ cup tomato sauce
- ⅓ cup cider vinegar
- ¼ cup oil
- 1 envelope GOOD SEASONS Zesty Italian Salad Dressing Mix
- 1 tablespoon hot pepper sauce or to taste
- 2 pounds chicken wings, separated at joints, tips discarded

MIX tomato sauce, vinegar, oil, salad dressing mix and pepper sauce in large bowl. Reserve ¼ cup marinade; refrigerate. Add chicken to bowl; toss to coat. Cover. Refrigerate 4 hours to marinate. Drain.

HEAT broiler. Place chicken on rack of broiler pan. Broil 4 inches from heat 16 to 20 minutes or until chicken is cooked through, turning and brushing occasionally with reserved ¼ cup marinade. Discard any remaining marinade.

Makes about 1½ dozen

Prep Time: 10 minutes
Cooking Time: 20 minutes

Clockwise from top: Pita Crisps (page 8), Sausage-Stuffed Mushrooms (page 9), Chicken Nuggets (page 8), Tangy Chicken Wings, Spicy Sweet 'n Sour Sauce (page 8)

Chicken Nuggets

1 pound boneless skinless
    chicken breasts, cut into
    1-inch chunks
1 envelope SHAKE 'N BAKE
    Seasoning and Coating
    Mixture—Original Recipe
    for Chicken
Spicy Sweet 'n Sour Sauce
    (see recipe this page)

HEAT oven to 400°F.

COAT chicken as directed on
package.

BAKE 15 to 20 minutes or until
chicken is cooked through. Serve
with Spicy Sweet 'n Sour Sauce for
dipping.
                Makes about 3 dozen

Prep Time: 5 minutes
Cooking Time: 20 minutes

Italian Chicken Nuggets: Prepare
as directed above, adding ¼ cup
(1 ounce) grated Parmesan cheese
to coating mixture before coating
chicken.

Chicken Fingers: Prepare as
directed above, using chicken
breasts cut into strips. Makes about
2 dozen.

---

*Greet guests coming in from
blustery weather with mugs of hot
buttered rum, cider or mulled
wine sweetened with rich
LOG CABIN Syrup.*

Spicy Sweet 'n Sour Sauce

¾ cup apricot preserves
⅓ cup prepared GOOD
    SEASONS Honey Mustard
    Salad Dressing
1 tablespoon hot pepper sauce
1 tablespoon soy sauce

MIX apricot preserves, salad
dressing, pepper sauce and soy
sauce in medium bowl until well
blended. Serve as a dipping sauce
for chicken nuggets, chicken
wings, egg rolls or breaded
vegetables.   *Makes 1¼ cup*

Prep Time: 5 minutes

Pita Crisps

½ cup (1 stick) margarine or
    butter, melted
1 envelope GOOD SEASONS
    Italian Salad Dressing Mix
4 large pita breads, each split
    into 2 circles

HEAT oven to 350°F.

MIX margarine and salad dressing
mix in small bowl until well
blended. Brush or drizzle on pita
circles. Cut each pita circle into
4 wedges. Arrange in single layer
on cookie sheets.

BAKE 10 to 12 minutes or until
crisp.   *Makes 3*

Prep Time: 5 minutes
Cooking Time: 15 minutes

Sausage-Stuffed Mushrooms

24 large mushroom caps
 3 tablespoons margarine or butter, melted, divided
¼ pound bulk pork sausage, crumbled
¼ cup chopped green onions
 1 cup STOVE TOP Cornbread Stuffing Mix in the Canister
½ cup hot water
¼ cup toasted chopped walnuts
½ teaspoon garlic powder
¼ teaspoon pepper
¼ teaspoon dried thyme leaves
¼ cup (1 ounce) grated Parmesan cheese

HEAT oven to 375°F.

CLEAN mushroom caps with damp paper towel. Brush mushroom caps with 2 tablespoons of the margarine. Place mushroom caps, stem-side up, in greased 13×9-inch baking dish; set aside.

BROWN sausage and onions in large skillet on medium heat. Remove from heat. Stir in stuffing mix, water, walnuts, remaining 1 tablespoon margarine, garlic powder, pepper and thyme until well mixed. Spoon evenly into mushroom caps. Sprinkle with cheese.

BAKE 10 to 12 minutes or until heated through.

Makes 2 dozen

Prep Time: 15 minutes
Cooking Time: 15 minutes

Pizza Bruschetta

 1 loaf Italian bread, cut into ¼-inch slices
 1 cup prepared GOOD SEASONS Italian *or* Zesty Italian Salad Dressing, divided
 1 cup (4 ounces) shredded mozzarella cheese
 4 ounces sliced pepperoni, halved (optional)
 1 large tomato, chopped
 1 medium green pepper, chopped
 2 mushrooms, sliced
 6 pitted ripe olives, sliced
¼ cup chopped green onions

HEAT oven to 450°F.

ARRANGE bread slices in single layer on cookie sheets. Brush with ½ cup of the dressing. Bake 5 minutes or until golden brown.

MIX cheese, pepperoni, tomato, pepper, mushrooms, olives and onions in medium bowl. Add remaining ½ cup dressing; toss to mix well. Spoon onto bread slices. Serve immediately.

Makes about 2 dozen

Prep Time: 15 minutes
Cooking Time: 5 minutes

Spinach Dip

1 cup KRAFT Real Mayonnaise
1 cup sour cream
1 envelope GOOD SEASONS
   Italian Salad Dressing Mix
1 package (10 ounces) frozen
   chopped spinach, thawed,
   well drained
1 can (8 ounces) water
   chestnuts, drained,
   chopped
½ small red pepper, chopped

MIX mayonnaise, sour cream and
salad dressing mix in medium bowl
until well blended. Stir in spinach,
water chestnuts and pepper.

SERVE with vegetable dippers or
chips. Store leftover dip in
refrigerator.
Makes about 3¼ cups

Prep Time: 10 minutes

Confetti Dip

1 cup sour cream
1 envelope GOOD SEASONS
   Italian *or* Zesty Italian
   Salad Dressing Mix
¼ cup finely chopped
   cucumber
¼ cup finely chopped onions
¼ cup finely chopped green
   pepper
¼ cup finely chopped red
   pepper

MIX sour cream and salad dressing
mix in medium bowl until well
blended. Stir in cucumber, onion
and peppers.

SERVE with vegetable dippers,
bread sticks or crackers. Store
leftover dip in refrigerator.
Makes about 1¾ cups

Prep Time: 10 minutes

Hot Clam Dip

1 package (8 ounces)
   PHILADELPHIA BRAND
   Cream Cheese, softened
¼ cup milk
½ cup KRAFT Real Mayonnaise
1 envelope GOOD SEASONS
   Italian Salad Dressing Mix
2 cans (7½ ounces *each*)
   minced clams, drained
¾ cup chopped green, red
   and/or yellow pepper
½ cup (2 ounces) shredded
   cheddar cheese
¼ cup (1 ounce) grated
   Parmesan cheese

HEAT oven to 375°F.

MIX cream cheese and milk in
large bowl with wire whisk until
smooth. Stir in mayonnaise and
salad dressing mix until well
blended.

STIR in clams, peppers and
cheeses. Spoon into 1-quart baking
dish.

BAKE 20 minutes or until heated
through. Serve hot with crackers,
French bread slices or vegetable
dippers.
Makes about 3½ cups

Prep Time: 10 minutes
Cooking Time: 20 minutes

---

*Dips can be made and used
immediately. Or, make ahead for
extra convenience.*

---

*Clockwise from top left: Spinach Dip,
Confetti Dip, Hot Clam Dip*

Bean and Rice Soup

2 slices bacon, cut into small
   pieces
1 celery stalk, chopped
1 small onion, chopped
4 cups water
1 can (16 ounces) pinto beans,
   undrained
1 can (16 ounces) small white
   beans, undrained
1 can (8 ounces) tomato sauce
1 teaspoon garlic powder
1 teaspoon salt
¼ teaspoon pepper
1 cup MINUTE Original Rice,
   uncooked

COOK and stir bacon, celery and
onion in 4-quart saucepan on
medium heat until bacon is crisp
and vegetables are tender.

STIR in water, beans, tomato sauce,
garlic powder, salt and pepper.
Cover. Bring to boil.

STIR in rice; cover. Remove from
heat. Let stand 5 minutes. Stir.

Makes 8 servings

Prep Time: 10 minutes
Cooking Time: 20 minutes

Bean and Rice Soup

Chunky Chicken Rice Soup

1 teaspoon oil
6 ounces boneless skinless
    chicken breasts, cut into
    ½-inch cubes (about 1 cup)
2 cans (13¾ ounces *each*)
    chicken broth
1 package (10 ounces) frozen
    mixed vegetables, thawed
1 cup water
½ teaspoon poultry seasoning
¼ teaspoon pepper
1 cup MINUTE Original Rice,
    uncooked
1 tablespoon chopped fresh
    parsley

HEAT oil in large saucepan on medium-high heat. Add chicken; cook and stir until browned.

STIR in broth, vegetables, water, poultry seasoning and pepper. Bring to boil. Reduce heat to low; cover and simmer 5 minutes.

STIR in rice and parsley; cover. Remove from heat. Let stand 5 minutes. Stir.

Makes 6 servings

Prep Time: 10 minutes
Cooking Time: 15 minutes

Hearty Minestrone

1 can (28 ounces) crushed
    tomatoes
2 cans (13¾ ounces *each*)
    chicken broth
1 cup water
1 can (16 ounces) white
    kidney beans, drained
1 package (10 ounces) frozen
    mixed vegetables
1 cup shredded cabbage
½ teaspoon dried oregano
    leaves
½ teaspoon salt
¼ teaspoon pepper
1 cup MINUTE Original Rice,
    uncooked

BRING tomatoes, broth and water to boil in large saucepan on medium-high heat.

STIR in beans, vegetables, cabbage, oregano, salt and pepper. Return to boil. Reduce heat to low; cover and simmer 5 minutes.

STIR in rice; cover. Remove from heat. Let stand 5 minutes. Stir.

Makes 10 servings

Prep Time: 10 minutes
Cooking Time: 15 minutes

Herb Crostini

24 slices (¼ inch thick) French
    bread (1 loaf)
    Olive oil
 1 container (15 ounces) ricotta
    cheese
 1 envelope GOOD SEASONS
    Italian Salad Dressing Mix
24 fresh basil leaves
 1 jar (7 ounces) roasted red
    peppers, drained, cut into
    strips

HEAT oven to 450°F.

ARRANGE bread slices in single
layer on cookie sheets. Brush with
oil. Bake 5 to 8 minutes or until
golden brown. Cool.

MIX cheese and salad dressing mix
in small bowl until well blended.

SPREAD about 1 tablespoon
cheese mixture on each toasted
bread slice. Top with basil leaf and
pepper strip. Serve immediately.
                    Makes 2 dozen

Prep Time: 10 minutes
Cooking Time: 10 minutes

◆

*A great spread for toasted French
bread slices or pita wedges: Mix
1 envelope GOOD SEASONS Salad
Dressing Mix with 1 stick softened
margarine or butter.*

◆

Black Bean Salsa

 1 envelope GOOD SEASONS
    Garlic & Herb Salad
    Dressing Mix
 1 can (16 ounces) black beans,
    rinsed, drained
 1 package (10 ounces) frozen
    corn, thawed
 1 tomato, chopped
 ¼ cup chopped red onion
 ¼ cup lime juice
 2 tablespoons chopped
    cilantro or fresh parsley
 ½ teaspoon minced fresh
    jalapeno pepper (optional)
 ¼ teaspoon ground cumin

MIX salad dressing mix, beans,
corn, tomato, onion, lime juice,
cilantro, jalapeno pepper and
cumin in medium bowl until
well blended. Cover. Refrigerate
15 minutes.

SERVE with tortilla chips. Store
leftover salsa in the refrigerator.
                Makes about 5 cups

Prep Time: 30 minutes

◆

*Create a savory cheese log: Cut an
8-ounce package of cream cheese
in half lengthwise, then roll each
half in GOOD SEASONS Italian,
Zesty Italian or Garlic & Herb
Salad Dressing Mix.*

◆

Shrimp and Corn Chowder

Shrimp and Corn Chowder

2 teaspoons oil
1 medium onion, chopped
1 celery stalk, sliced
½ cup chopped ham
3 tablespoons flour
½ teaspoon pepper
¼ teaspoon dried thyme leaves
3 cups milk
1 package (16 ounces) frozen sweet corn, thawed
1 can (13¾ ounces) reduced sodium chicken broth
1 cup MINUTE Brown Rice, uncooked
¼ pound shrimp, cleaned, coarsely chopped
2 tablespoons chopped fresh parsley

HEAT oil in 4-quart saucepan on medium-high heat. Add onion, celery and ham; cook and stir until vegetables are tender. Stir in flour, pepper and thyme.

STIR in milk, corn and broth. Cover. Bring to boil, stirring occasionally.

STIR in rice and shrimp. Return to boil. Reduce heat to low; cover and simmer 5 minutes. Remove from heat. Let stand 5 minutes. Stir in parsley.   *Makes 8 servings*

Prep Time: 10 minutes
Cooking Time: 20 minutes

Easy Main Dish Meals

If you're like most busy people, you probably feel there aren't enough hours in the day to get your work done, run your household and still put a home-cooked meal on the table. Now you can serve delicious dinners every night without spending all day making them!

Consider Mapley Mustard Chicken, Spaghetti Sauce Bolognese, or a kid's favorite, Mac & Stuff. All of these delectable recipes and more are gathered in this collection of Easy Main Dish Meals. Home-cooked meals have never tasted so good, nor have they been so quick and easy to prepare!

Linguine with Clam Sauce

3 dozen medium clams
1 bottle (8 ounces) clam juice
¼ cup olive oil
1 tablespoon vinegar
1 envelope GOOD SEASONS Zesty Italian, Italian *or* Garlic & Herb Salad Dressing Mix
2 tablespoons chopped fresh basil
1 tablespoon chopped fresh parsley
8 ounces linguine or spaghetti, cooked, drained

SCRUB and rinse clams; drain well.

BRING clam juice, oil, vinegar and salad dressing mix to boil in large skillet on medium-high heat. Add clams. Reduce heat to low; cover and simmer 5 to 8 minutes or until clams open. Discard any unopened clams. Stir in basil and parsley.

SERVE clam sauce over hot linguine.   *Makes 4 servings*

Prep Time: 10 minutes
Cooking Time: 15 minutes

Linguine with Clam Sauce

Sloppy Joes with Rice

Sloppy Joes with Rice

¾ **pound ground beef**
1 **small onion, sliced**
1 **small red or green pepper,**
   cut into strips
1 **cup barbecue sauce**
1½ **cups water**
½ **teaspoon salt**
1½ **cups MINUTE Original Rice,**
   uncooked
   Shredded cheddar cheese
   (optional)

BROWN meat, onion and pepper in large skillet on medium heat. Drain. Stir in barbecue sauce. Bring to boil. Reduce heat to low; cover and simmer 5 minutes.

MEANWHILE, bring water and salt to boil in medium saucepan. Stir in rice; cover. Remove from heat. Let stand 5 minutes. Fluff with fork. Serve meat mixture over rice. Sprinkle with cheese.

Makes 4 servings

Prep Time: 5 minutes
Cooking Time: 15 minutes

Honey Mustard Chicken Kabobs

⅓ cup orange juice *or* dry white wine
⅓ cup oil
1 envelope GOOD SEASONS Honey Mustard Salad Dressing Mix
1 pound boneless skinless chicken breasts, cut into 1-inch chunks
1 medium onion, cut into chunks
1 medium green pepper, cut into chunks
1 medium red pepper, cut into chunks

MIX orange juice, oil and salad dressing mix in large bowl. Reserve ¼ cup marinade; refrigerate. Add chicken, onion and peppers to bowl; toss to coat. Cover. Refrigerate 2 hours to marinate. Drain.

HEAT broiler. Arrange chicken, onion and peppers alternately on skewers. Place kabobs on rack of broiler pan. Broil 3 inches from heat 15 minutes or until chicken is cooked through, turning and brushing occasionally with reserved ¼ cup marinade. Discard any remaining marinade.
Makes 4 servings

Prep Time: 10 minutes
Cooking Time: 15 minutes

Cinnamon-Spiced Chicken

1 envelope SHAKE 'N BAKE Seasoning and Coating Mixture—Original Recipe for Chicken
½ teaspoon ground cinnamon
6 boneless skinless chicken breast halves
¼ cup apple jelly
2 tablespoons LOG CABIN Syrup

HEAT oven to 400°F.

MIX coating mixture and cinnamon in shaker bag. Coat chicken as directed on package.

BAKE 15 minutes on ungreased or foil-lined 15×10-inch metal baking pan. Mix apple jelly and syrup in small bowl until well blended. Drizzle over chicken. Bake 5 minutes or until chicken is cooked through.   *Makes 6 servings*

Prep Time: 5 minutes
Cooking Time: 20 minutes

Try this easy maple-flavored barbecue sauce for ribs, chops or burgers. Mix ¾ cup barbecue sauce, ¼ cup LOG CABIN Syrup, 1 tablespoon minced onion and 1 teaspoon lemon juice. Tangy . . . and quick!

Sweet 'n Sour Pork Chops

1 can (8¼ ounces) chunk
   pineapple in syrup,
   undrained
¼ cup cider vinegar
1 tablespoon cornstarch
1 medium green pepper, cut
   into chunks
8 pork chops, ½ inch thick
1 envelope SHAKE 'N BAKE
   Seasoning and Coating
   Mixture—Barbecue Recipe
   for Pork

HEAT oven to 425°F.

DRAIN pineapple, reserving syrup.
Mix vinegar and 1 tablespoon of
the syrup; set aside. Mix cornstarch
and remaining syrup in medium
bowl until smooth. Stir in
pineapple and pepper. Pour into
13×9-inch baking pan.

MOISTEN chops with vinegar
mixture, shaking off excess liquid.
Coat as directed on package. Place
on pineapple mixture.

BAKE 25 minutes or until cooked
through. Serve with pineapple
mixture.   *Makes 8 servings*

Prep Time: 5 minutes
Cooking Time: 25 minutes

Sweet 'n Sour Chicken: Prepare as
directed above, using Barbecue
Recipe for Chicken and
substituting 8 boneless skinless
chicken breast halves for pork
chops.

Mapley Mustard Chicken

¾ cup LOG CABIN LITE Reduced
   Calorie Syrup
¼ cup spicy brown mustard
2 tablespoons lemon juice
1 tablespoon vegetable oil
4 boneless skinless chicken
   breast halves

MIX syrup, mustard and lemon
juice in small bowl.

HEAT oil in large skillet on
medium-high heat. Add chicken;
brown on both sides. Pour syrup
mixture over chicken. Reduce heat
to low; simmer 15 minutes or until
chicken is cooked through.

SERVE chicken mixture over hot
cooked noodles, if desired.
                    Makes 4 servings

Prep Time: 5 minutes
Cooking Time: 25 minutes

*Top to bottom: Sweet 'n Sour Pork
Chops, Mapley Mustard Chicken
Chicken and Shrimp Kabobs (page 22)*

Chicken and Shrimp Kabobs

⅓ cup dry white wine *or* water
⅓ cup oil
1 envelope GOOD SEASONS Italian *or* Mild Italian Salad Dressing Mix
½ pound boneless skinless chicken breasts, cut into 1-inch chunks
½ pound shrimp, cleaned
8 medium mushroom caps
1 medium red pepper, cut into chunks
1 medium green pepper, cut into chunks

MIX wine, oil and salad dressing mix in large bowl. Reserve ¼ cup marinade; refrigerate. Add chicken, shrimp, mushrooms and peppers to bowl; toss to coat. Cover. Refrigerate 2 hours to marinate. Drain.

HEAT broiler. Arrange chicken, shrimp, mushrooms and peppers alternately on skewers. Place kabobs on rack of broiler pan. Broil 2 inches from heat 10 to 12 minutes or until chicken is cooked through and shrimp turn pink, turning and brushing occasionally with reserved ¼ cup marinade. Discard any remaining marinade.

Makes 4 servings

Prep Time: 10 minutes
Cooking Time: 15 minutes

Mac & Stuff

1 package (7¼ ounces) KRAFT Macaroni and Cheese Dinner
1¼ cups water
1 cup frozen green peas, thawed
4 hot dogs, sliced
2 tablespoons margarine or butter
2 cups STOVE TOP Chicken Flavor Stuffing Mix in the Canister

PREPARE Dinner as directed on package.

MEANWHILE, bring water, peas, hot dogs and margarine to boil in large saucepan. Stir in stuffing mix just to moisten; cover. Remove from heat. Let stand 5 minutes.

STIR stuffing mixture lightly into prepared Dinner. Serve immediately.

Makes 4 servings

Prep Time: 10 minutes
Cooking Time: 15 minutes

For a quick glaze for ham or pork roasts, drizzle LOG CABIN Syrup over the roast during the last 25 to 30 minutes of roasting time.

Tuna, Rice and Biscuits

Tuna, Rice and Biscuits

- 1 tablespoon margarine or butter
- 1 cup chopped onions
- 2½ cups milk
- 1 can (10¾ ounces) condensed cream of celery soup
- 1 package (10 ounces) frozen mixed vegetables, thawed
- ½ teaspoon dill weed
- ⅛ teaspoon pepper
- 1½ cups MINUTE Original Rice, uncooked
- 1 can (12½ ounces) tuna, drained, flaked
- 1 package (7½ ounces) refrigerated buttermilk biscuits

HEAT oven to 450°F.

MELT margarine in large skillet on medium-high heat. Add onion; cook and stir until tender. Stir in milk, soup, vegetables, dill and pepper. Bring to boil.

STIR in rice and tuna. Pour into greased 2-quart casserole. Top with biscuits.

BAKE 8 to 10 minutes or until biscuits are golden brown.
Makes 6 servings

Prep Time: 5 minutes
Cooking Time: 20 minutes

Chicken, Rice and Biscuits:
Prepare as directed above, substituting 2 cups chopped cooked chicken for tuna.

Lemon Parsley Chicken and Rice

1 tablespoon oil
4 boneless skinless chicken
  breast halves
1½ cups chicken broth
1½ cups MINUTE Brown Rice,
  uncooked
2 tablespoons chopped fresh
  parsley
1 teaspoon grated lemon peel
⅛ teaspoon pepper
3 tablespoons toasted whole
  almonds

HEAT oil in large skillet on medium-high heat. Add chicken; brown on both sides.

STIR in broth. Bring to boil.

STIR in rice. Return to boil. Reduce heat to low; cover and simmer 5 minutes. Remove from heat. Stir in parsley, lemon peel and pepper; cover. Let stand 5 minutes. Fluff rice with fork. Sprinkle with almonds.   *Makes 4 servings*

Prep Time: 10 minutes
Cooking Time: 20 minutes

Apricot Glazed Chicken

1 envelope SHAKE 'N BAKE
  Seasoning Coating
  Mixture—Original Recipe
  for Chicken
½ teaspoon ground ginger
6 boneless skinless chicken
  breast halves
¼ cup apricot preserves
1 tablespoon soy sauce

HEAT oven to 400°F.

MIX coating mixture and ginger in shaker bag. Coat chicken as directed on package.

BAKE 15 minutes on ungreased or foil-lined 15×10-inch metal baking pan. Mix preserves and soy sauce in small bowl until well blended. Drizzle over chicken. Bake 5 minutes or until chicken is cooked through.   *Makes 6 servings*

Prep Time: 5 minutes
Cooking Time: 20 minutes

Spaghetti Sauce Bolognese

2 tablespoons oil
¾ pound ground beef
¾ cup chopped onions
1 can (28 ounces) crushed
  tomatoes with puree
1 envelope GOOD SEASONS
  Italian Salad Dressing Mix
2 teaspoons sugar (optional)

HEAT oil in large saucepan on medium-high heat. Add meat and onions; cook and stir until meat is browned. Drain.

STIR in tomatoes, salad dressing mix and sugar. Bring to boil. Reduce heat to low; cover and simmer 10 minutes, stirring occasionally. Serve over hot cooked pasta, if desired.
     Makes 4 to 6 servings

Prep Time: 5 minutes
Cooking Time: 15 minutes

Cranberry-Orange Chicken

1 envelope SHAKE 'N BAKE
   Seasoning and Coating
   Mixture—Original Recipe
   for Chicken
1 tablespoon grated orange
   peel
6 boneless skinless chicken
   breast halves
1 cup whole berry cranberry
   sauce
2 tablespoons orange juice

HEAT oven to 400°F.

MIX coating mixture and orange
peel in shaker bag. Coat chicken as
directed on package.

BAKE 15 minutes on ungreased or
foil-lined 15×10-inch metal baking
pan. Mix cranberry sauce and
orange juice in small bowl until
well blended. Spoon over chicken.
Bake 5 minutes or until chicken is
cooked through.

Makes 6 servings

Prep Time: 5 minutes
Cooking Time: 20 minutes

---

*Zip up ho-hum chicken with this
quick marinade. Prepare GOOD
SEASONS Italian or Honey
Mustard Dressing. Reserve ¼ cup
dressing; refrigerate. Pour
remaining dressing over chicken
pieces (about 2½ pounds); toss
to coat. Cover and refrigerate
overnight. Drain chicken; discard
any remaining marinade. Bake
or grill chicken as usual,
basting with reserved ¼ cup
dressing. Fantastic!*

Penne with Asparagus and Shrimp

1 container (16 ounces) lowfat
   cottage cheese
¼ cup reduced fat sour cream
2 tablespoons chopped fresh
   parsley
1 envelope GOOD SEASONS
   Garlic & Herb Salad
   Dressing Mix
2 teaspoons olive oil
6 asparagus spears, cut into
   1-inch pieces
½ pound medium shrimp,
   cleaned
1 small red pepper, cut into
   thin strips
8 ounces penne *or* ziti pasta,
   cooked, drained

MIX cottage cheese, sour cream,
parsley and salad dressing mix in
small bowl until well blended.

HEAT oil in large nonstick skillet
on medium heat. Add asparagus;
cook and stir 3 minutes. Add
shrimp and red pepper; cover.
Cook 5 minutes or until shrimp are
pink and vegetables are tender-
crisp, stirring occasionally.

TOSS hot pasta with cheese and
shrimp mixtures in large bowl
until well mixed. Serve
immediately.

Makes 4 servings

Prep Time: 15 minutes
Cooking Time: 15 minutes

One-Dish Dinners

*W*ho says a good meal has to require a lot of time and effort? One way to simplify daily meal preparation is to make use of this delicious collection of one-dish dinners—the easiest of all suppers. Everything goes together in one skillet or casserole dish, making preparation simple and cleanup a snap.

Even after a busy day, you and your family can enjoy a home-cooked dinner brimming with robust flavor. Pork Chops with Apples and Stuffing, Salsa Rice and Black Beans, and Ham and Sweet Potato Skillet are a few enticing examples. Once prepared, all you need are a few simple accompaniments, such as a tossed salad and beverage, for a great tasting meal that's on the table in 30 minutes or less.

Chicken with Stuffing and Peaches

1 can (16 ounces) sliced peaches in heavy syrup, undrained
2 tablespoons oil
4 boneless skinless chicken breast halves
1 tablespoon brown sugar
1 tablespoon cider vinegar
⅛ teaspoon ground allspice
2 cups STOVE TOP Chicken Flavor Stuffing Mix in the Canister

DRAIN peaches, reserving syrup. Add water to syrup to measure 1 cup; set aside.

HEAT oil in large skillet on medium-high heat. Add chicken; brown on both sides.

STIR in measured liquid, sugar, vinegar and allspice. Bring to boil. Reduce heat to low; cover and simmer 8 minutes or until chicken is cooked through. Move chicken to side of skillet.

STIR in stuffing mix and peaches; cover. Remove from heat. Let stand 5 minutes.   *Makes 4 servings*

Prep Time: 5 minutes
Cooking Time: 20 minutes

Chicken with Stuffing and Peaches

Herbed Tomato Pork Chops and Stuffing

1 tablespoon oil
4 pork chops, ½ inch thick
1 can (8 ounces) stewed
    tomatoes
1 can (8 ounces) tomato sauce
1 medium green pepper,
    chopped
½ teaspoon dried oregano
    leaves
¼ teaspoon ground pepper
2 cups STOVE TOP Chicken
    Flavor Stuffing Mix in the
    Canister
1 cup (4 ounces) shredded
    mozzarella cheese, divided

HEAT oil in large skillet on medium-high heat. Add chops; brown on both sides.

STIR in tomatoes, tomato sauce, green pepper, oregano and ground pepper. Bring to boil. Reduce heat to low; cover and simmer 15 minutes or until chops are cooked through. Remove chops from skillet.

STIR stuffing mix and ½ cup of the cheese into skillet. Return chops to skillet. Sprinkle with remaining ½ cup cheese; cover. Remove from heat. Let stand 5 minutes.

Makes 4 servings

Prep Time: 5 minutes
Cooking Time: 25 minutes

Herbed Tomato Pork Chops and Stuffing

Chicken and Primavera Stuffing

3 tablespoons margarine or butter, divided
6 boneless skinless chicken breast halves
1½ cups water
¼ teaspoon pepper
2½ cups assorted cut-up vegetables, such as broccoli flowerets, red pepper strips, zucchini slices
3 cups STOVE TOP Chicken Flavor Stuffing Mix in the Canister

MELT 1 tablespoon of the margarine in large skillet on medium-high heat. Add chicken; brown on both sides.

STIR in water, remaining 2 tablespoons margarine and pepper. Bring to boil. Reduce heat to low; cover and simmer 5 minutes. Add vegetables; cover and simmer 5 minutes or until chicken is cooked through and vegetables are tender-crisp. Remove chicken from skillet.

STIR stuffing mix into skillet just to moisten. Return chicken to skillet; cover. Remove from heat. Let stand 5 minutes.
                    Makes 6 servings

Prep Time: 10 minutes
Cooking Time: 20 minutes

Skillet Chicken Divan

1 tablespoon oil
1 pound boneless skinless chicken breasts, cut into strips
1 can (10¾ ounces) condensed cream of chicken soup
1 package (10 ounces) frozen broccoli spears, thawed
1 cup water
1 tablespoon dry sherry
1½ cups MINUTE Original Rice, uncooked
½ cup (2 ounces) shredded cheddar cheese

HEAT oil in large skillet on medium-high heat. Add chicken; cook and stir until browned.

STIR in soup, broccoli, water and sherry. Bring to boil.

STIR in rice; cover. Remove from heat. Let stand 5 minutes. Stir. Sprinkle with cheese; cover. Let stand 3 minutes or until cheese is melted.   *Makes 4 servings*

Prep Time: 5 minutes
Cooking Time: 15 minutes

Here's an easy topping, right from your pantry shelf, for baked casseroles. Just sprinkle STOVE TOP Stuffing Mix in the Canister onto your favorite casserole before baking. This zesty topping adds crispness as well as great flavor!

Chicken Brown Rice Primavera

- 1 tablespoon oil
- ¾ pound boneless skinless chicken breasts, cut into strips
- 2 cloves garlic, minced
- 1½ cups chicken broth
- 1 cup broccoli flowerets
- ½ cup diagonally sliced carrot
- ½ cup sliced yellow squash
- ½ medium red pepper, cut into strips
- ¼ teaspoon ground pepper
- 1½ cups MINUTE Brown Rice, uncooked
- ¼ cup (1 ounce) grated Parmesan cheese

HEAT oil in large skillet on medium-high heat. Add chicken and garlic; cook and stir until chicken is lightly browned.

STIR in broth, broccoli, carrot, squash, red pepper and ground pepper. Bring to boil.

STIR in rice. Return to boil. Reduce heat to low; cover and simmer 5 minutes. Remove from heat and stir; cover. Let stand 5 minutes. Stir in cheese.

Makes 4 servings

Prep Time: 10 minutes
Cooking Time: 15 minutes

Skillet Sausage and Peppers

- 1 pound bulk Italian sausage
- 1 medium onion, cut into wedges
- 1 small green pepper, cut into strips
- 1 small red pepper, cut into strips
- 1 can (8 ounces) tomato sauce
- 1 can (8 ounces) whole tomatoes, undrained
- ½ teaspoon dried oregano leaves
- 2 cups STOVE TOP Chicken Flavor Stuffing Mix in the Canister

BROWN sausage in large skillet on medium-high heat. Stir in onion, peppers, tomato sauce, tomatoes and oregano. Bring to boil. Reduce heat to low; cover and simmer 5 minutes or until vegetables are tender-crisp.

STIR in stuffing mix just to moisten; cover. Remove from heat. Let stand 5 minutes.

Makes 4 servings

Prep Time: 15 minutes
Cooking Time: 15 minutes

Counter-clockwise from top right: Pork Chops with Apples and Stuffing (page 33), Skillet Sausage and Peppers, Chicken Brown Rice Primavera

Salsa Rice and Black Beans

1¼ cups water
1½ cups MINUTE Brown Rice, uncooked
1 can (16 ounces) black beans, rinsed, drained
1 large tomato, chopped
1 can (4 ounces) chopped green chilies, undrained
1 tablespoon chopped cilantro or fresh parsley
1 tablespoon lime juice
⅛ teaspoon hot pepper sauce
  Suggested Garnishes: light sour cream, lime slices, cilantro or fresh parsley

BRING water to boil in large saucepan on medium-high heat.

STIR in rice, beans, tomato and chilies. Return to boil. Reduce heat to low; cover and simmer 5 minutes. Remove from heat.

STIR in cilantro, lime juice and pepper sauce; cover. Let stand 5 minutes. Stir. Garnish as desired.

Makes 4 servings

Prep Time: 10 minutes
Cooking Time: 20 minutes

Pork Chops with Apples and Stuffing

4 pork chops, ½ inch thick
  Salt and pepper
1 tablespoon oil
2 medium apples, cored, cut into 8 wedges
1 cup apple juice
2 cups STOVE TOP Cornbread Stuffing Mix in the Canister
¼ cup chopped pecans

SPRINKLE chops with salt and pepper. Heat oil in large skillet on medium-high heat. Add chops and apples; cook until chops are browned on both sides.

STIR in apple juice. Bring to boil. Reduce heat to low; cover and simmer 8 minutes or until chops are cooked through. Remove chops from skillet.

STIR stuffing mix and pecans into skillet. Return chops to skillet; cover. Remove from heat. Let stand 5 minutes.   *Makes 4 servings*

Prep Time: 10 minutes
Cooking Time: 20 minutes

Salsa Rice and Black Beans

Easy Beef and Rice Stew

  2 tablespoons flour
  ½ teaspoon salt
  ¼ teaspoon pepper
  1 pound boneless beef top
      round, cut into ¾-inch
      chunks
  1 tablespoon oil
  2 medium carrots, diagonally
      sliced
  1 medium onion, coarsely
      chopped
  1 jar (4½ ounces) sliced
      mushrooms, drained
  1 can (14½ ounces) whole
      tomatoes, undrained,
      coarsely chopped
  1 can (10¼ ounces) beef gravy
  ¼ cup burgundy or other dry
      red wine
  1½ cups MINUTE Original Rice,
      uncooked

MIX flour, salt and pepper in large bowl. Add meat; toss to coat.

HEAT oil in large skillet on medium-high heat. Add meat; cook and stir until browned. Add carrots, onion and mushrooms; cook and stir 2 minutes.

STIR in tomatoes, gravy and wine. Bring to boil. Reduce heat to low; cover and simmer 10 minutes.

STIR in rice; cover. Remove from heat. Let stand 5 minutes. Stir.
Makes 4 servings

Prep Time: 10 minutes
Cooking Time: 20 minutes

Ham and Sweet Potato Skillet

  2 tablespoons margarine or
      butter
  ¾ cup LOG CABIN Syrup
  ¼ teaspoon dry mustard
  1 teaspoon whole cloves
  1 ham steak (1 pound)
  2 medium apples, thinly sliced
  2 cans (16 to 17 ounces *each*)
      sweet potatoes, drained

MELT margarine in large skillet on medium heat. Stir in syrup and mustard. Cook 5 minutes, stirring frequently.

INSERT cloves into one side of ham steak. Place in skillet, clove-side down.

COOK ham steak 3 minutes; turn over. Add apples and sweet potatoes. Cover partially with lid. Cook 5 minutes or until apples are tender, basting sweet potatoes and apples occasionally with syrup mixture.   *Makes 4 servings*

Prep Time: 10 minutes
Cooking Time: 15 minutes

Top to bottom: Ham and Sweet Potato Skillet, Easy Beef and Rice Stew

Orange Glazed Chicken and Stuffing

2 tablespoons margarine or butter
4 boneless skinless chicken breast halves
2 medium carrots, thinly sliced
½ cup orange juice
½ cup water
4 tablespoons orange marmalade, divided
2 cups STOVE TOP Chicken Flavor Stuffing Mix in the Canister

MELT margarine in large skillet on medium-high heat. Add chicken; brown on both sides.

STIR in carrots, orange juice, water and 2 tablespoons of the marmalade. Bring to boil. Reduce heat to low; cover and simmer 8 minutes or until chicken is cooked through and carrots are tender. Move chicken to side of skillet. Spoon remaining 2 tablespoons marmalade over chicken.

STIR in stuffing mix just to moisten; cover. Remove from heat. Let stand 5 minutes.

Makes 4 servings

Prep Time: 5 minutes
Cooking Time: 20 minutes

Festive Chicken and Stuffing

3 tablespoons margarine or butter, divided
1¼ pounds boneless skinless chicken breasts, cut into 1-inch pieces
1½ cups sliced mushrooms
1½ cups water
1 medium carrot, shredded
1 small zucchini, shredded
1 tablespoon lemon juice
1 teaspoon dill weed
¼ teaspoon pepper
3 cups STOVE TOP Chicken Flavor Stuffing Mix in the Canister

MELT 1 tablespoon of the margarine in large skillet on medium-high heat. Add chicken and mushrooms; cook and stir until chicken is browned.

STIR in water and remaining 2 tablespoons margarine. Bring to boil. Reduce heat to low; cover and simmer 5 minutes.

STIR in carrot, zucchini, lemon juice, dill and pepper. Stir in stuffing mix just to moisten; cover. Remove from heat. Let stand 5 minutes. *Makes 6 servings*

Prep Time: 15 minutes
Cooking Time: 15 minutes

Cheeseburger Rice

1 pound ground beef
1 small onion, chopped
1½ cups water
½ cup catsup
2 tablespoons prepared
   mustard
½ teaspoon salt
⅛ teaspoon pepper
1½ cups MINUTE Original Rice,
   uncooked
1 cup (4 ounces) shredded
   cheddar cheese

BROWN beef and onion in large
skillet on medium-high heat.
Drain.

STIR in water, catsup, mustard, salt
and pepper. Bring to boil.

STIR in rice; cover. Remove from
heat. Let stand 5 minutes. Stir.
Sprinkle with cheese; cover. Let
stand 3 minutes or until cheese is
melted.   *Makes 4 servings*

Prep Time: 5 minutes
Cooking Time: 15 minutes

◆

*Try this easy supper salad. Toss
leftover cooked chicken or turkey
cubes, ham and cheese strips,
chilled cooked pasta, chopped
green pepper and tomato with
prepared GOOD SEASONS
Salad Dressing.*

◆

Barbecued Chicken and Stuffing

2 tablespoons oil
4 boneless skinless chicken
   breast halves
1 medium onion, thinly sliced
1 can (11 ounces) whole
   kernel corn with sweet
   peppers, drained
1 cup water
⅔ cup barbecue sauce
2 cups STOVE TOP Chicken
   Flavor Stuffing Mix in the
   Canister

HEAT oil in large skillet on
medium-high heat. Add chicken
and onion; cook until chicken is
browned on both sides.

STIR in corn, water and barbecue
sauce. Bring to boil. Reduce heat to
low; cover and simmer 8 minutes
or until chicken is cooked through.
Move chicken to side of skillet.

STIR in stuffing mix just to
moisten; cover. Remove from heat.
Let stand 5 minutes.
        Makes 4 servings

Prep Time: 5 minutes
Cooking Time: 15 minutes

Microwave in Minutes

*M*icrowave cooking is a great timesaver for today's cook. Remember when supper had to bake in the oven or simmer on the stove for hours? Well, not anymore!

Microwavable recipes such as those in this chapter are the heart of easy home-cooked family meals. Here, we've streamlined the preparation time, pared down the ingredients and put the microwave to work. You can turn out delicious meals and side dishes such as Chicken with Corn and Peppers, Ratatouille Rice or Mapley Microwaved Beans in just minutes. We've even included a selection of great tasting kids' favorites sure to satisfy even the most finicky eater.

Mapley Microwaved Beans

3 slices bacon, chopped
1 small onion, chopped
2 cans (16 ounces *each*) pork and beans
½ cup LOG CABIN Syrup
2 tablespoons catsup
1 tablespoon prepared mustard
½ teaspoon hot pepper sauce (optional)

MIX bacon and onion in 1½-quart microwavable casserole. Cover loosely with wax paper.

MICROWAVE on HIGH 5 minutes. Drain. Stir in beans, syrup, catsup, mustard and pepper sauce. Cover loosely with wax paper.

MICROWAVE 10 minutes, stirring halfway through cooking time.
Makes 8 servings

Prep Time: 5 minutes
Cooking Time: 15 minutes

Top to bottom: Mapley Microwaved Beans, Brown Rice Almondine (page 40)

Brown Rice Almondine

1½ cups MINUTE Brown Rice, uncooked
1¼ cups chicken broth
1 medium onion, chopped
1 tablespoon lemon juice
1 tablespoon margarine or butter
2 teaspoons chopped fresh dill *or* ½ teaspoon dill weed
1 clove garlic, minced
1 cup frozen cut green beans, thawed
2 tablespoons toasted sliced almonds

MIX rice, broth, onion, lemon juice, margarine, dill and garlic in 2-quart microwavable casserole. Cover.

MICROWAVE on HIGH 5 minutes. Stir in beans. Cover.

MICROWAVE 5 minutes. Let stand 5 minutes. Stir in almonds.

Makes 6 servings

Prep Time: 5 minutes
Cooking Time: 15 minutes

Pierce whole, unpeeled vegetables, such as potatoes or yams, with a fork to keep them from bursting while cooking in the microwave.

Microwave Lemon Chicken and Rice

1 pound boneless skinless chicken breasts, cut into ½-inch chunks
1½ cups chicken broth
1½ cups MINUTE Original Rice, uncooked
1 medium red pepper, cut into strips
1 medium zucchini, thinly sliced
½ teaspoon grated lemon peel
3 tablespoons fresh lemon juice
2 tablespoons margarine or butter
1 tablespoon cornstarch
½ teaspoon garlic powder

MIX chicken, broth, rice, pepper, zucchini, lemon peel and juice, margarine, cornstarch and garlic powder in 2-quart microwavable casserole. Cover.

MICROWAVE on HIGH 10 minutes or until chicken is cooked through, stirring halfway through cooking time. Let stand 5 minutes. Stir.

Makes 4 servings

Prep Time: 10 minutes
Cooking Time: 15 minutes

Ratatouille Rice

2 cans (14½ ounces *each*)
    stewed tomatoes
1 large onion, chopped
1 cup chopped peeled eggplant
1 small green pepper, chopped
1 small zucchini, chopped
1 jar (4½ ounces) sliced
    mushrooms, drained
½ teaspoon ground pepper
1½ cups MINUTE Original Rice,
    uncooked
¼ cup (1 ounce) grated
    Parmesan cheese
¼ cup chopped fresh parsley

MIX tomatoes, onion, eggplant,
green pepper, zucchini,
mushrooms and ground pepper in
2-quart microwavable casserole.
Cover.

MICROWAVE on HIGH 6 minutes,
stirring halfway through cooking
time. Stir in rice. Cover.

MICROWAVE 8 minutes or until
vegetables are tender. Let stand 5
minutes. Stir in cheese and parsley.
Makes 8 servings

Prep Time: 10 minutes
Cooking Time: 20 minutes

---

*Stir vegetable pieces or rotate
vegetables halfway through
microwave cooking time to allow
more even cooking of pieces.*

Microwave Baked Apples

4 large baking apples, cored
½ cup LOG CABIN Syrup *or*
    LOG CABIN LITE Reduced
    Calorie Syrup
3 tablespoons margarine or
    butter, melted
½ teaspoon ground cinnamon

CUT thin slice off bottom of each
apple to form a flat surface. Place
apples in microwavable casserole.

MIX syrup, margarine and
cinnamon in small bowl. Spoon
into center of apples. Cover loosely
with wax paper.

MICROWAVE on HIGH 10 minutes
or until apples are tender, rotating
dish halfway through cooking time.
Makes 4 servings

Prep Time: 5 minutes
Cooking Time: 10 minutes

---

*Loosely cover foods with wax
paper, plastic wrap or a casserole
lid to allow steam to escape
when microwaving.*

Chunky Chili Casserole

2 cups STOVE TOP Chicken Flavor *or* Cornbread Stuffing Mix in the Canister
½ cup hot water
½ pound ground beef
1 small onion, chopped
1 can (15 ounces) chili with beans
1½ cups (6 ounces) shredded cheddar cheese, divided
½ cup frozen sweet corn, thawed
¼ cup sliced pitted ripe olives
Sour cream

MIX stuffing mix and hot water in 2-quart microwavable casserole. Spread evenly in casserole.

MIX meat and onion in large microwavable bowl. Cover loosely with wax paper.

MICROWAVE on HIGH 4 minutes or until meat is no longer pink. Drain. Stir in chili, 1 cup of the cheese, corn and olives. Spoon over stuffing. Cover loosely with wax paper.

MICROWAVE 10 minutes, rotating casserole halfway through cooking time. Let stand 5 minutes. Sprinkle with remaining ½ cup cheese. Serve with sour cream.

Makes 4 servings

Prep Time: 5 minutes
Cooking Time: 20 minutes

Note: Recipe can also be prepared in 4 individual 1½-cup microwavable dishes. Microwave each dish on HIGH 3 minutes or until heated through.

Fiesta Pie

3 eggs
¾ cup milk
2 cups STOVE TOP Chicken Flavor *or* Cornbread Stuffing Mix in the Canister
1½ cups chopped cooked chicken
1 large tomato, chopped
1 can (4 ounces) chopped green chilies, drained
¼ cup chopped green onions
Suggested Garnishes: tomato wedges, sour cream, sliced green onions

BEAT eggs in large bowl; stir in milk. Stir in stuffing mix, chicken, tomato, chilies and chopped onions until well mixed. Spoon into greased 9-inch microwavable pie plate. Cover loosely with wax paper.

MICROWAVE on HIGH 5 minutes. Stir thoroughly to completely mix center and outside edges; smooth top. Cover.

MICROWAVE 4 minutes or until center is no longer wet. Let stand 5 minutes. Garnish as desired.

Makes 4 to 6 servings

Prep Time: 10 minutes
Cooking Time: 15 minutes

Top to bottom: Fiesta Pie, Chunky Chili Casserole, Surfin' Tuna Casserole (page 44)

Surfin' Tuna Casserole

   3 eggs
¾ cup milk
   2 cups STOVE TOP Chicken
      Flavor Stuffing Mix in the
      Canister
1½ cups (6 ounces) shredded
      colby/Monterey Jack
      cheese, divided
   1 cup frozen green peas,
      thawed
   1 can (6⅛ ounces) tuna,
      drained, flaked
½ cup condensed cream of
      mushroom soup
¼ cup chopped green onions
   2 tablespoons chopped
      pimiento

BEAT eggs in large bowl; stir in milk. Stir in stuffing mix, 1 cup of the cheese, peas, tuna, soup, onions and pimento until well mixed. Spoon into greased 9-inch microwavable pie plate. Cover loosely with wax paper.

MICROWAVE on HIGH 5 minutes. Stir thoroughly to completely mix center and outside edges; smooth top. Cover.

MICROWAVE 5 minutes or until center is no longer wet. Sprinkle with remaining ½ cup cheese; cover. Let stand 5 minutes.
                    Makes 4 to 6 servings

Prep Time: 10 minutes
Cooking Time: 15 minutes

Chicken with Corn and Peppers

   1 package (10 ounces) frozen
      sweet corn, thawed
   1 medium green pepper, cut
      into chunks
   1 medium red pepper, cut into
      chunks
   1 cup salsa
   4 boneless skinless chicken
      breast halves
   1 envelope SHAKE 'N BAKE
      Seasoning and Coating
      Mixture—Barbecue Recipe
      for Chicken

MIX corn, peppers and salsa in 2-quart microwavable casserole. Coat chicken with coating mixture as directed on package. Place on vegetable mixture. Cover loosely with wax paper.

MICROWAVE on HIGH 10 to 12 minutes or until chicken is cooked through, rotating casserole halfway through cooking time.
                    Makes 4 servings

Prep Time: 10 minutes
Cooking Time: 15 minutes

Tomato, Bacon and Cheese Supper

1 medium onion, chopped
2 tablespoons margarine or
     butter
1 cup ricotta cheese
1 cup milk
3 eggs, well beaten
3 cups STOVE TOP Chicken
     Flavor *or* Cornbread
     Stuffing Mix in the
     Canister
1 cup (4 ounces) shredded
     Swiss cheese, divided
2 large tomatoes, chopped
8 slices bacon, crisply cooked,
     crumbled
¼ teaspoon pepper

PLACE onion and margarine in 3-quart microwavable casserole. Cover loosely with wax paper.

MICROWAVE on HIGH 3 minutes. Stir in ricotta cheese, milk and eggs. Stir in stuffing mix, ¾ cup of the Swiss cheese, tomatoes, bacon and pepper until well mixed. Cover loosely with wax paper.

MICROWAVE 10 minutes, stirring halfway through cooking time. Sprinkle with remaining ¼ cup Swiss cheese. Let stand 5 minutes.

Makes 6 servings

Prep Time: 5 minutes
Cooking Time: 20 minutes

Tomato, Bacon and Cheese Supper

Chicken and Zucchini Casserole

Chicken and Zucchini Casserole

1¼ cups hot water
  3 tablespoons margarine or butter, divided
  3 cups STOVE TOP Chicken Flavor *or* Cornbread Stuffing Mix in the Canister
  ¾ pound boneless skinless chicken breasts, cubed
  2 medium zucchini, cut into ½-inch pieces
1½ cups (6 ounces) shredded cheddar cheese
  1 can (8 ounces) water chestnuts, drained, halved (optional)
  ½ teaspoon dried basil leaves
  ¼ teaspoon pepper

MIX water and 2 tablespoons of the margarine in large bowl until margarine is melted. Stir in stuffing mix just to moisten.

PLACE chicken, zucchini and remaining 1 tablespoon margarine in 3-quart microwavable casserole. Cover loosely with wax paper.

MICROWAVE on HIGH 4 minutes, stirring halfway through cooking time. Stir in prepared stuffing, cheese, water chestnuts, basil and pepper until well mixed. Cover.

MICROWAVE 10 minutes, stirring halfway through cooking time. Let stand 5 minutes.

Makes 6 servings

Prep Time: 10 minutes
Cooking Time: 20 minutes

Easy Spinach Pie

3 eggs
¾ cup milk
2 cups STOVE TOP Chicken
    Flavor Stuffing Mix in the
    Canister
1 package (10 ounces) frozen
    chopped spinach, thawed,
    well drained
1 cup cubed ham
¾ cup cottage cheese
⅓ cup sliced green onions
¼ teaspoon garlic powder
⅓ cup (about 1½ ounces)
    shredded cheddar cheese

BEAT eggs in large bowl; stir in
milk. Stir in stuffing mix, spinach,
ham, cottage cheese, onions and
garlic powder until well mixed.
Spoon into greased 9-inch
microwavable pie plate. Cover
loosely with wax paper.

MICROWAVE on HIGH 5 minutes.
Stir thoroughly to completely mix
center and outside edges; smooth
top. Cover.

MICROWAVE 5 minutes or until
center is no longer wet. Sprinkle
with cheddar cheese; cover. Let
stand 5 minutes.

Makes 6 servings

Prep Time: 10 minutes
Cooking Time: 15 minutes

*For a vibrant finish, toss 2 cups
hot cooked vegetables with
2 tablespoons prepared GOOD
SEASONS Salad Dressing Mix.*

Cheesy Rice and Broccoli

1 package (10 ounces) frozen
    chopped broccoli
1 cup water
½ pound VELVEETA Cheese
    Spread, cubed
1½ cups MINUTE Original Rice,
    uncooked

PLACE broccoli and water in
2-quart microwavable casserole.
Cover.

MICROWAVE on HIGH 3 minutes.
Break apart broccoli with fork. Stir
in cheese spread and rice. Cover.

MICROWAVE 8 to 10 minutes or
until rice is tender and mixture is
heated through, stirring halfway
through cooking time.

Makes 6 servings

Prep Time: 5 minutes
Cooking Time: 15 minutes

*Deli-roasted turkey slices become
a satisfying meal: Layer prepared
STOVE TOP Stuffing Mix and
sliced turkey in individual
microwavable dishes; top with
prepared chicken gravy.
Microwave until heated through.*

Southwest Adventures

*F*or a delicious change of pace and taste, try out this collection of Southwestern recipes sure to deliver big-time Mexican taste in just minutes. Contemporary Southwestern flavors inspired these colorful meals that are as easy to serve as they are fun to eat.

For those evenings when you can't spare time for cooking—whether you're helping the kids with homework or getting a head start on the laundry—rely on surefire family pleasers such as Skillet Fajitas, Chicken Hash Ranchero or Sierra Chicken and Rice.

Only a few simple ingredients such as tortillas, prepared salsa, chili powder and Monterey Jack cheese are needed in order to add Southwestern flavor to these easy recipes.

Chile Rellenos-Style Chicken

6 boneless skinless chicken breast halves
1 envelope SHAKE 'N BAKE Seasoning and Coating Mixture—Hot & Spicy Recipe for Chicken
½ cup (2 ounces) shredded cheddar or Monterey Jack cheese*
1 can (4 ounces) chopped green chilies, drained
Salsa (optional)

*Or use ¼ cup of each cheese.

HEAT oven to 400°F.

COAT chicken with coating mixture as directed on package.

BAKE 20 minutes on ungreased or foil-lined 15×10-inch metal baking pan. Mix cheese and chilies. Spoon over chicken. Bake 5 minutes or until chicken is cooked through and cheese is melted. Serve with salsa.   *Makes 4 servings*

Prep Time: 5 minutes
Cooking Time: 25 minutes

Chile Rellenos-Style Chicken

Baked Pork Fajitas Mexicana

1 medium onion, sliced
1 medium green pepper, cut into strips
1 medium red pepper, cut into strips
2 tablespoons oil
1 tablespoon lime *or* lemon juice
½ teaspoon ground cumin
8 boneless pork chops, ½ inch thick
1 envelope SHAKE 'N BAKE Seasoning and Coating Mixture—Hot & Spicy *or* Original Recipe for Pork
  Flour tortillas, heated
  Suggested Toppings: guacamole, salsa, sour cream

HEAT oven to 425°F.

MIX onion, peppers, oil, lime juice and cumin in 13×9-inch baking pan until well mixed. Coat chops as directed on package. Place on pepper mixture.

BAKE 20 minutes or until chops are cooked through. Cut chops into slices. Fill tortillas with sliced pork and pepper mixture. Serve with Suggested Toppings.

Makes 8 servings

Prep Time: 10 minutes
Cooking Time: 20 minutes

For a creamy Ranchero Dip in just minutes, mix 1 cup <u>each</u> salsa and sour cream with 1 envelope GOOD SEASONS Garlic and Herbs Salad Dressing Mix.

Easy Chicken Rice Tacos

1 tablespoon margarine or butter
½ pound ground chicken or turkey
1 small onion, chopped
1 package (1¼ ounces) taco seasoning mix
1¼ cups water
1 can (8 ounces) tomato sauce
1½ cups MINUTE Original Rice, uncooked
1 can (16 ounces) kidney beans, drained (optional)
16 taco shells, heated
  Suggested Toppings: shredded cheddar cheese, shredded lettuce, chopped tomatoes, sour cream

MELT margarine in large skillet on medium-high heat. Add chicken, onion and seasoning mix; cook and stir until chicken is no longer pink.

STIR in water and tomato sauce. Bring to boil. Reduce heat to low; cover and simmer 5 minutes.

STIR in rice and beans; cover. Remove from heat. Let stand 5 minutes. Fill each taco shell with chicken mixture. Serve with Suggested Toppings.

Makes 16 tacos or 8 servings

Prep Time: 5 minutes
Cooking Time: 15 minutes

Top to bottom: Baked Pork Fajitas Mexicana, Easy Chicken Rice Tacos

Skillet Fajitas

½ cup oil
¼ cup lime juice
2 tablespoons water
1 envelope GOOD SEASONS
    Zesty Italian Salad
    Dressing Mix
2 teaspoons hot pepper sauce
½ teaspoon ground cumin
⅛ teaspoon ground pepper
1 beef flank steak (1 pound),
    cut into thin strips
1 large onion, cut into ¼-inch
    slices
1 large green pepper, cut into
    strips
1 large red pepper, cut into
    strips
    Flour tortillas, heated
    Suggested Toppings:
    guacamole, salsa, sour
    cream

MIX oil, lime juice, water, salad
dressing mix, pepper sauce, cumin
and ground pepper in large bowl
until well blended. Add meat,
onion and peppers; toss to coat. Let
stand 10 minutes at room
temperature. Drain.

HEAT large skillet on medium-high
heat. Add ½ of the meat mixture;
cook and stir until meat is
browned. Remove. Repeat with
remaining meat mixture. Fill
tortillas with meat mixture. Serve
with suggested toppings.
                    Makes 6 servings

Prep Time: 15 minutes
Cooking Time: 10 minutes

Chicken Hash Ranchero

2 cups STOVE TOP Cornbread
    or Chicken Flavor Stuffing
    Mix in the Canister
1 cup hot water
1½ cups chopped cooked
    chicken or turkey
1 cup chopped red and/or
    green pepper
½ cup frozen sweet corn,
    thawed
¼ cup sliced green onions
2 tablespoons chopped
    cilantro or fresh parsley
1 teaspoon hot pepper sauce
2 tablespoons oil

MIX stuffing mix and hot water in
large bowl just to moisten. Stir in
chicken, peppers, corn, onions,
cilantro and pepper sauce until
well mixed.

HEAT oil in large nonstick skillet
on medium-high heat. Spread
chicken mixture evenly in skillet.
Cook 10 minutes or until lightly
browned, dividing into sections
and turning over to brown on both
sides.   *Makes 4 servings*

Prep Time: 5 minutes
Cooking Time: 15 minutes

Counter-clockwise from top right:
Skillet Fajitas, Chicken Hash
Ranchero, Southwest Pork and
Dressing (page 54)

Southwest Pork and Dressing

1 pound boneless pork, cut into 1-inch strips
2 teaspoons chili powder
¼ cup margarine or butter
½ cup diagonally sliced green onions
1½ cups water
1 cup frozen sweet corn, thawed
1 can (4 ounces) chopped green chilies, drained
3 cups STOVE TOP Cornbread Stuffing Mix in the Canister
1¼ cups (5 ounces) shredded Monterey Jack cheese, divided

TOSS meat with chili powder. Melt margarine in large skillet on medium-high heat. Add meat and onions; cook and stir until meat is browned.

STIR in water, corn and chilies. Bring to boil. Stir in stuffing mix and ¾ cup of the cheese. Remove from heat. Sprinkle with remaining ½ cup cheese. Cover. Let stand 5 minutes.

Makes 4 to 6 servings

Prep Time: 10 minutes
Cooking Time: 15 minutes

Mexican Rice: Bring 1 package (10 ounces) frozen corn, 1 cup chicken broth and 1 cup salsa to boil in medium saucepan. Stir in 1½ cups uncooked MINUTE Rice; cover. Remove from heat; let stand 5 minutes.

Chili with Rice

1 pound lean ground beef
1 small green pepper, chopped
1 package (1¾ ounces) chili seasoning mix
1½ cups water
1 can (15¼ ounces) kidney beans, drained
1 can (8 ounces) tomato sauce
1 can (7 ounces) whole kernel corn, drained (optional)
1 can (4 ounces) chopped green chilies, drained
1½ cups MINUTE Original Rice, uncooked
¼ cup (1 ounce) shredded cheddar cheese

COOK and stir meat, pepper and seasoning mix in large skillet on medium-high heat until meat is browned.

STIR in water, beans and tomato sauce. Bring to boil. Reduce heat to low; cover and simmer 10 minutes, stirring occasionally.

STIR in corn and chilies. Return to boil.

STIR in rice; cover. Remove from heat. Let stand 5 minutes. Stir. Sprinkle with cheese.

Makes 6 servings

Prep Time: 10 minutes
Cooking Time: 20 minutes

Barbecued pork and chicken get Southwestern flavor when you mix 1 tablespoon chili powder with SHAKE 'N BAKE Barbecue Coating Mixes before coating pork chops or chicken pieces.

Sierra Chicken and Rice

Sierra Chicken and Rice

1 tablespoon oil
1 pound boneless skinless
   chicken breasts, cut into
   1-inch chunks
1 large onion, chopped
1 can (15¼ ounces) kidney
   beans, drained
1 jar (12 ounces) chunky salsa
1 cup frozen sweet corn,
   thawed
½ cup chicken broth
1½ cups MINUTE Original Rice,
   uncooked
½ cup sour cream
   Suggested Garnishes:
      additional sour cream,
      chopped tomatoes, sliced
      pitted ripe olives, sliced
      green onions, tortilla chips

HEAT oil in large skillet on medium-high heat. Add chicken and onion; cook and stir until chicken is cooked through.

STIR in beans, salsa, corn and broth. Bring to boil.

STIR in rice; cover. Remove from heat. Let stand 5 minutes. Stir in sour cream. Garnish as desired.
Makes 4 to 6 servings

Prep Time: 10 minutes
Cooking Time: 15 minutes

Add 1 can (4 ounces) chopped green chilies, drained, to each 6-serving quantity of prepared STOVE TOP Cornbread Stuffing for extra zip.

International Intrigue

*B*ecause Americans favor foreign foods, this chapter is devoted to delightful recipes from around the world. Whether you're looking for a quick and easy entree for the family or an elegant recipe for a special occasion, you're sure to find it here.

Traditionally, many of these classic international recipes require a lot of preparation time. Our renditions have been adapted to make use of the simplest techniques possible. As a plus, they feature products that make the most of a few ingredients—and your time.

Find enticing family suppers with continental flair, like Skillet Chicken Cordon Bleu, Quick Paella and Chicken Piccata. With these recipes, the world of delectable possibilities is enormous.

Hungarian-Style Pork Chops

1 envelope SHAKE 'N BAKE
    Seasoning and Coating
    Mixture—Original Recipe
    for Pork
1 tablespoon paprika
8 pork chops, ½ inch thick
1 cup sour cream
2 tablespoons chopped green
    pepper
2 tablespoons chopped tomato
½ teaspoon paprika

HEAT oven to 425°F.

MIX coating mixture and 1 tablespoon paprika in shaker bag. Coat chops as directed on package.

BAKE 25 minutes or until chops are cooked through. Mix sour cream, pepper, tomato and ½ teaspoon paprika until well blended. Serve with chops.
Makes 4 servings

Prep Time: 5 minutes
Cooking Time: 25 minutes

Top to bottom: Easy Chicken Cacciatore (page 58), Chicken Piccata (page 58), Hungarian-Style Pork Chops

Easy Chicken Cacciatore

2 tablespoons oil
4 boneless skinless chicken
   breast halves
1 medium onion, sliced
1 medium green pepper, cut
   into strips
1 cup sliced mushrooms
1 envelope GOOD SEASONS
   Italian, Mild Italian *or*
   Zesty Italian Salad
   Dressing Mix
1 can (28 ounces) crushed
   tomatoes with puree

HEAT oil in large skillet on
medium-high heat. Add chicken,
onion, pepper and mushrooms;
cook and stir until chicken is
browned on both sides.

SPRINKLE salad dressing mix over
chicken mixture. Stir in tomatoes.
Bring to boil. Reduce heat to low;
cover and simmer 15 minutes,
stirring occasionally.

SERVE chicken mixture over hot
cooked pasta, if desired.
Makes 4 servings

Prep Time: 5 minutes
Cooking Time: 25 minutes

◆

*Stir 1 envelope GOOD SEASONS
Italian Salad Dressing Mix into
1 container (16 ounces) sour
cream or lowfat yogurt. Spoon
over hot baked potatoes.*

◆

Chicken Piccata

4 boneless skinless chicken
   breast halves
½ cup flour
2 to 4 tablespoons oil
¾ cup chicken broth
¼ cup lemon juice
2 tablespoons grated
   Parmesan cheese
1 tablespoon flour
1 envelope GOOD SEASONS
   Italian Salad Dressing Mix
   Hot cooked MINUTE Original
   Rice

CUT chicken in half lengthwise;
pound to ¼-inch thickness. Coat
chicken using ½ cup flour. Shake
off excess.

HEAT 2 tablespoons oil in large
skillet on medium-high heat. Add
½ of the chicken; brown on both
sides. Remove. Repeat with
remaining chicken, adding
remaining oil as needed. Remove
chicken from skillet; keep warm.

MIX broth, lemon juice, cheese,
1 tablespoon flour and salad
dressing mix in small bowl until
well blended. Stir into skillet.
Stirring constantly, bring to boil;
boil 1 minute. Serve with chicken
and rice. *Makes 4 servings*

Prep Time: 10 minutes
Cooking Time: 15 minutes

Pork and Cabbage Rice

   2 teaspoons oil
   ¾ pound boneless pork, cut
      into strips
   ½ cup red cabbage strips
   ½ teaspoon caraway seed
      (optional)
   ½ teaspoon pepper
1½ cups water
   ½ cup applesauce
   2 tablespoons cider vinegar
1½ cups MINUTE Brown Rice,
      uncooked
   1 tart apple, cored, sliced

HEAT oil in large skillet on medium-high heat. Add meat; cook and stir until lightly browned. Add cabbage, caraway seed and pepper; cook and stir 1 minute.

STIR in water, applesauce and vinegar. Bring to boil.

STIR in rice and apple. Reduce heat to low; cover and simmer 5 minutes. Remove from heat and stir; cover. Let stand 5 minutes. Stir.

Makes 4 servings

Prep Time: 10 minutes
Cooking Time: 20 minutes

Pork and Cabbage Rice

Quick Paella

1 tablespoon oil
1 pound hot Italian sausage, cut into 1-inch pieces
2 cloves garlic, minced
1 tablespoon cornstarch
1 can (13¾ ounces) chicken broth
1 package (10 ounces) frozen peas and pearl onions, thawed
½ pound medium shrimp, cleaned
1 can (8 ounces) stewed tomatoes
1½ cups MINUTE Original Rice, uncooked
⅛ teaspoon saffron *or* ground turmeric (optional)

HEAT oil in large skillet on medium-high heat. Add sausage and garlic; cook and stir until sausage is browned.

MIX cornstarch and broth until smooth. Stir into skillet. Add vegetables, shrimp and tomatoes; cook and stir until mixture thickens and comes to boil.

STIR in rice and saffron; cover. Remove from heat. Let stand 5 minutes. Stir.

Makes 6 servings

Prep Time: 10 minutes
Cooking Time: 15 minutes

Italian-Style Chicken

6 boneless skinless chicken breast halves
¼ cup spicy brown mustard
1 envelope SHAKE 'N BAKE Seasoning and Coating Mixture—Original *or* Italian Recipe for Chicken
6 slices hard salami
6 slices provolone or mozzarella cheese

HEAT oven to 400°F.

BRUSH chicken on both sides with mustard. Coat with coating mixture as directed on package.

BAKE 15 minutes. Top each chicken piece with 1 slice of salami and cheese. Bake 5 minutes or until chicken is cooked through and cheese is melted.

Makes 6 servings

Prep Time: 5 minutes
Cooking Time: 25 minutes

Try an Italian twist on potato salad. Combine 1 envelope GOOD SEASONS Italian Salad Dressing Mix with 1 cup mayonnaise. Add sliced cooked potatoes (about 6 cups), sliced celery and ripe olives, as desired; toss lightly to coat.

Orange Glazed Chicken Stir-Fry

1 tablespoon oil
¾ pound boneless skinless chicken breasts, cut into strips
1 tablespoon cornstarch
1½ cups chicken broth
½ cup orange juice
2 tablespoons reduced sodium soy sauce
1 tablespoon brown sugar
½ teaspoon ground ginger
½ teaspoon garlic powder
1 package (10 ounces) frozen baby carrots, thawed, drained
1 package (8 ounces) frozen snap peas, thawed, drained
1½ cups MINUTE Brown Rice, uncooked

HEAT oil in large skillet on medium-high heat. Add chicken; stir-fry until lightly browned.

MIX cornstarch, broth, juice, soy sauce, sugar, ginger and garlic powder in medium bowl until smooth. Stir into skillet. Stirring constantly, bring to boil on medium heat; boil 1 minute.

STIR in carrots, snap peas and rice. Return to boil. Reduce heat to low; cover and simmer 5 minutes. Remove from heat. Let stand 5 minutes. Stir.

Makes 4 servings

Prep Time: 5 minutes
Cooking Time: 20 minutes

Curried Chicken

1 envelope SHAKE 'N BAKE Seasoning and Coating Mixture—Hot & Spicy Recipe for Chicken
1¼ teaspoons curry powder, divided
6 boneless skinless chicken breast halves
2 bananas, thinly sliced
¼ cup toasted slivered almonds
2 tablespoons brown sugar

HEAT oven to 400°F.

MIX coating mixture and 1 teaspoon of the curry powder in shaker bag. Coat chicken as directed on package.

BAKE 15 minutes. Mix bananas, almonds, sugar and remaining ¼ teaspoon curry powder in medium bowl. Spoon over chicken. Bake 5 minutes or until chicken is cooked through.

Makes 6 servings

Prep Time: 5 minutes
Cooking Time: 20 minutes

For Parmesan Rice: Prepare MINUTE Rice, stirring ½ teaspoon dried basil leaves into the boiling water. Sprinkle with grated Parmesan cheese before serving.

Orange Glazed Chicken Stir-Fry

Skillet Chicken Cordon Bleu

1 tablespoon margarine or
    butter
¾ pound boneless skinless
    chicken breasts, cut into
    strips
2 ounces boiled ham, cut into
    strips (about ½ cup)
1 can (10¾ ounces) condensed
    cream of chicken soup
1 package (10 ounces) frozen
    cut green beans, thawed
1 cup water
1 tablespoon Dijon mustard
1½ cups MINUTE Original Rice,
    uncooked
⅔ cup (about 3 ounces)
    shredded Swiss cheese

MELT margarine in large skillet on medium-high heat. Add chicken and ham; cook and stir until chicken is browned.

STIR in soup, beans, water and mustard. Bring to boil.

STIR in rice; cover. Remove from heat. Let stand 5 minutes. Stir. Sprinkle with cheese; cover. Let stand 3 minutes or until cheese is melted.   *Makes 4 servings*

Prep Time: 10 minutes
Cooking Time: 15 minutes

Caribbean Jerk Chicken

½ cup oil
¼ cup red wine vinegar
1 envelope GOOD SEASONS
    Italian Salad Dressing Mix
2 tablespoons brown sugar
2 tablespoons soy sauce
1 teaspoon ground allspice
1 teaspoon ground cinnamon
1 teaspoon dried thyme leaves
½ to ¾ teaspoon ground red
    pepper
8 boneless skinless chicken
    breast halves

MIX oil, vinegar, salad dressing mix, sugar, soy sauce, allspice, cinnamon, thyme and pepper in large baking dish. Reserve ¼ cup of the marinade. Add chicken to baking dish; turn to coat well. Let stand 5 minutes at room temperature. Drain.

HEAT broiler. Place chicken on rack of broiler pan. Broil 3 inches from heat 16 to 20 minutes or until chicken is cooked through, turning and brushing frequently with reserved ¼ cup marinade. Discard any remaining marinade. Serve chicken with hot cooked rice, if desired.

Makes 6 to 8 servings

Prep Time: 10 minutes
Cooking Time: 20 minutes

Teriyaki Beef

3 tablespoons soy sauce
1 tablespoon dry sherry
2 teaspoons brown sugar
1½ teaspoons garlic powder
1 teaspoon ground ginger
¾ pound beef flank steak, cut into thin strips
1 tablespoon oil
2 cups broccoli flowerets
1 small red pepper, cut into thin strips
4 teaspoons cornstarch
1 cup beef broth
1½ cups water
1½ cups MINUTE Original Rice, uncooked

MIX soy sauce, sherry, brown sugar, garlic powder and ginger in medium bowl. Add meat; toss to coat well. Let stand 10 minutes to marinate.

HEAT oil in large skillet on medium-high heat. Add meat; stir-fry until browned. Add vegetables; stir-fry until tender-crisp.

MIX cornstarch and broth until smooth. Gradually stir into skillet. Stirring constantly, bring to boil on medium heat; boil 1 minute.

MEANWHILE, bring water to boil in medium saucepan. Stir in rice; cover. Remove from heat. Let stand 5 minutes or until liquid is absorbed. Fluff with fork. Serve meat mixture over rice.

Makes 4 servings

Prep Time: 15 minutes
Cooking Time: 15 minutes

Chicken Parmesan

¼ cup seasoned dry bread crumbs
2 tablespoons grated Parmesan cheese
4 boneless skinless chicken breast halves
1 egg, beaten
2 tablespoons oil
1 can (14½ ounces) stewed tomatoes
1 can (8 ounces) tomato sauce
¼ teaspoon dried oregano leaves
1½ cups MINUTE Original Rice, uncooked
½ cup (2 ounces) shredded mozzarella cheese

MIX bread crumbs and Parmesan cheese. Dip chicken in egg, shaking off excess. Coat with crumb mixture.

HEAT oil in large skillet on medium-high heat. Add chicken; brown on both sides until cooked through. Remove from skillet. Drain on paper towels.

STIR tomatoes, tomato sauce and oregano into skillet. Bring to boil.

STIR in rice. Top with chicken. Sprinkle with mozzarella cheese; cover. Remove from heat. Let stand 5 minutes.   *Makes 4 servings*

Prep Time: 10 minutes
Cooking Time: 20 minutes

Savory Side Dishes & Simply Delicious Salads

*T*ransform the simplest meal into a sensational one with any of these savory side dishes or tempting salads. With just a few added ingredients, GOOD SEASONS Salad Dressing Mix, MINUTE Rice and STOVE TOP Stuffing Mix become something special.

Weekday dinners become a feast when you serve them with side dishes such as Pesto Rice with Peas, Fresh Vegetable Saute or Herb-Roasted Potatoes and Peppers.

For a gourmet touch, plan a salad made to order in a matter of minutes. Choose Mediterranean Pasta Salad or Farmer's Market Salad. Surprisingly easy to make, these appealing entree salads and refreshing side dish salads are ready to serve in just 30 minutes or less.

Italian Bread Salad

> 2 cups STOVE TOP Chicken Flavor Stuffing Mix in the Canister
> ½ cup hot water
> 2 medium tomatoes, chopped
> 1 small red onion, chopped
> ½ small cucumber, chopped
> ¼ cup olive oil
> 2 tablespoons red wine vinegar

MIX stuffing mix and hot water in large bowl just to moisten. Let stand 5 minutes. Stir in tomatoes, onion and cucumber.

MIX oil and vinegar in small bowl. Add to stuffing mixture; toss lightly. Serve immediately.
Makes 4 servings

Prep Time: 15 minutes

Clockwise from top: Italian Bread Salad, Creamy Bacon Rice (page 68), Savory Broiled Vegetables (page 68)

Creamy Bacon Rice

1½ cups water
¼ teaspoon salt
1½ cups MINUTE Original Rice,
   uncooked
½ cup (2 ounces) shredded
   cheddar cheese
½ cup sour cream
3 slices bacon, crisply cooked,
   crumbled
2 green onions, thinly sliced

BRING water and salt to boil in
medium saucepan.

STIR in rice; cover. Remove from
heat. Let stand 5 minutes. Stir in
cheese, sour cream, bacon and
onions.   *Makes 6 servings*

Prep Time: 10 minutes
Cooking Time: 10 minutes

---

*For a savory side dish to serve
with beef, prepare MINUTE Rice
with beef broth instead of water.
With chicken, use chicken broth
instead of the water. For extra
flavor, stir ½ teaspoon dried herb
or seasoning (oregano, thyme,
sage, curry or dill) into
the cooking water.*

Savory Broiled Vegetables

1 cup prepared GOOD
   SEASONS Italian,
   Garlic & Herb *or* Honey
   Mustard Salad Dressing
4 medium onions, cut into
   thick slices
2 small zucchini, halved
   lengthwise
2 medium red peppers,
   quartered

POUR dressing over vegetables in
large bowl. Let stand 15 minutes.
Drain, reserving ¼ cup dressing.

HEAT broiler. Place vegetables on
rack of broiler pan. Broil 4 inches
from heat 6 to 8 minutes or until
vegetables are browned on both
sides, turning and brushing
occasionally with reserved ¼ cup
dressing.   *Makes 4 servings*

Prep Time: 20 minutes
Cooking Time: 10 minutes

Streusel Topped Sweet Potatoes

Streusel Topped Sweet Potatoes

- **3 cans (16 to 17 ounces *each*)** sweet potatoes, drained, mashed
- **½ cup LOG CABIN Syrup**
- **1 teaspoon grated orange peel**
- **⅓ cup flour**
- **⅓ cup old-fashioned or quick-cooking oats, uncooked**
- **¼ cup firmly packed brown sugar**
- **¼ teaspoon ground cinnamon**
- **¼ cup (½ stick) margarine or butter**
- **¼ cup chopped pecans**

HEAT oven to 400°F.

MIX potatoes, syrup and orange peel until well blended. Spoon into 2-quart casserole; smooth top.

MIX flour, oats, sugar and cinnamon in medium bowl. Cut in margarine until coarse crumbs form. Stir in pecans. Sprinkle over potatoes.

BAKE 20 minutes or until potatoes are heated through.

Makes 8 to 10 servings

Prep Time: 10 minutes
Cooking Time: 20 minutes

Herb-Roasted Potatoes and Peppers

1 pound red potatoes, cut into
⅛-inch slices
1 small red pepper, cut into
chunks
1 small green pepper, cut into
chunks
1 small onion, cut into chunks
¼ cup prepared GOOD
SEASONS Italian *or*
Garlic & Herb Salad
Dressing

HEAT oven to 450°F.

MIX potatoes, peppers and onion
in shallow baking pan. Add
dressing; toss to coat.

BAKE 25 minutes or until potatoes
are tender, stirring occasionally.
Makes 4 servings

Prep Time: 5 minutes
Cooking Time: 25 minutes

Fresh Vegetable Saute

¼ cup olive oil
6 cups assorted cut-up
vegetables, such as
broccoli flowerets, green
beans, cauliflowerets,
sugar snap peas, pepper
strips, diagonally sliced
carrots, mushrooms,
onions, yellow squash and
zucchini
1 envelope GOOD SEASONS
Italian Salad Dressing Mix
¼ cup red wine vinegar

HEAT oil in large skillet on
medium-high heat. Add vegetables;
cook and stir until tender-crisp.

STIR in salad dressing mix and
vinegar; cook and stir until heated
through.
Makes 4 to 6 servings

Prep Time: 15 minutes
Cooking Time: 10 minutes

Brown Rice with Zucchini and Carrots

2 teaspoons margarine or
butter
1 small onion, chopped
½ cup shredded carrot
1¼ cups chicken broth
½ teaspoon dill weed
Dash pepper
1½ cups MINUTE Brown Rice,
uncooked
½ cup shredded zucchini

MELT margarine in medium
saucepan on medium-high heat.
Add onion and carrot; cook and stir
until onion is tender.

STIR in broth, dill and pepper.
Bring to boil.

STIR in rice. Return to boil.
Reduce heat to low; cover and
simmer 5 minutes. Remove from
heat. Stir in zucchini; cover. Let
stand 5 minutes. Fluff with fork.
Makes 6 servings

Prep Time: 10 minutes
Cooking Time: 15 minutes

*Counter-clockwise from top right:
Brown Rice with Zucchini and
Carrots, Fresh Vegetable Saute,
Herb-Roasted Potatoes and Peppers*

Farmer's Market Salad

2 cups cucumber chunks
2 cups sliced celery
2 cups green, red and/or
   yellow pepper chunks
2 cups cherry tomatoes,
   halved
1 cup sliced radishes
1 cup red onion chunks
1 cup prepared GOOD
   SEASONS Fat Free Italian *or*
   Zesty Herb Salad Dressing

MIX vegetables in large bowl. Add dressing; toss to coat.

SERVE immediately or refrigerate until ready to serve.

Makes 12 servings

Prep Time: 20 minutes

For a change of pace, experiment with different combinations of vinegars and oils when preparing your favorite GOOD SEASONS flavor.

Vinegar Variations—*Try apple cider, red wine, balsamic, raspberry or tarragon vinegar. Or, use fresh lemon juice, orange juice, grapefruit juice, lime juice or tomato juice instead of vinegar.*

Oil Options—*Use vegetable, canola, corn or safflower oil. Or, substitute olive oil for all or part of the oil you regularly use. For dressing prepared with olive oil, let refrigerated dressing reach room temperature before serving.*

Pesto Rice with Peas

1 can (13¾ ounces) chicken
   broth
1 package (10 ounces) frozen
   green peas, thawed
½ cup water
⅓ cup prepared pesto sauce
2¼ cups MINUTE Original Rice,
   uncooked
⅓ cup (about 1½ ounces)
   grated Parmesan cheese

BRING broth, peas, water and pesto sauce to boil in large saucepan.

STIR in rice; cover. Remove from heat. Let stand 5 minutes. Stir in cheese.   *Makes 8 servings*

Prep Time: 5 minutes
Cooking Time: 15 minutes

Applesauce Rice

1 cup applesauce
1 cup water
1 teaspoon margarine or
   butter
¼ teaspoon ground cinnamon
¼ teaspoon salt
1½ cups MINUTE Brown Rice,
   uncooked
1 small apple, chopped

BRING applesauce, water, margarine, cinnamon and salt to boil in medium saucepan.

STIR in rice; cover. Remove from heat. Let stand 5 minutes. Stir in apple.   *Makes 4 servings*

Prep Time: 5 minutes
Cooking Time: 10 minutes

Farmer's Market Salad

Mediterranean Pasta Salad

2½ cups (6 ounces) bow tie pasta
    or shell macaroni,
    uncooked
½ pound shrimp, cleaned,
    cooked, halved lengthwise
1 medium zucchini, sliced
1 medium carrot, cut into
    julienne strips
1 small red pepper, cut into
    strips
1 small green pepper, cut into
    strips
8 pitted ripe olives, sliced
½ cup (2 ounces) crumbled feta
    cheese *or* shredded
    mozzarella cheese
½ teaspoon crushed red pepper
1 cup prepared GOOD
    SEASONS Italian *or* Zesty
    Italian Salad Dressing

PREPARE pasta as directed on
package; drain. Rinse with cold
water; drain.

MIX pasta, shrimp, zucchini,
carrot, peppers, olives, cheese and
crushed red pepper in large bowl.
Add dressing; toss to coat.

SERVE immediately or refrigerate
until ready to serve.

Makes 4 to 6 servings

Prep Time: 25 minutes

Green Bean and Mozzarella Cheese Salad

2 cups fresh green beans,
    halved
6 plum tomatoes, sliced
1 package (8 ounces)
    mozzarella cheese, cut into
    ½-inch cubes
⅓ cup chopped fresh basil
⅛ teaspoon pepper
⅓ cup prepared GOOD
    SEASONS Zesty Italian
    Salad Dressing

COOK beans in enough boiling
water to cover in medium saucepan
4 minutes or until tender-crisp.
Drain. Rinse with cold water; drain.

MIX beans, tomatoes, cheese, basil
and pepper in large bowl. Add
dressing; toss to coat.

SERVE immediately or refrigerate
until ready to serve.

Makes 4 servings

Prep Time: 15 minutes

*Top to bottom: Mediterranean Pasta
Salad, Green Bean and Mozzarella
Cheese Salad, Tossed Orange Salad
(page 76)*

Tossed Orange Salad

1 envelope GOOD SEASONS
   Honey Mustard *or* Italian
   Salad Dressing Mix
8 cups torn mixed salad greens
4 oranges, sectioned
½ pound bacon, crisply
   cooked, crumbled
   (optional)
1 small red onion, thinly sliced
1 cup toasted pecan halves

PREPARE salad dressing mix as
directed on envelope. Refrigerate.

MIX salad greens, oranges, bacon,
onion and pecans in large bowl.
Add dressing; toss lightly. Serve
immediately.
   Makes 8 to 10 servings

Prep Time: 20 minutes

---

*To toast nuts for salads and side
dishes, spread nuts in a shallow
pan. Toast at 400°F for 8 to 10
minutes or until golden brown,
stirring frequently.*

Pasta Garden Salad

1 package (16 ounces) ridged
   mostaccioli, ziti *or*
   medium shell macaroni,
   uncooked
4 cups assorted cut-up
   vegetables, such as green
   beans, broccoli flowerets,
   red and yellow pepper
   strips, sliced yellow squash
   and zucchini
1 cup sliced pitted ripe olives
½ cup (2 ounces) grated
   Parmesan cheese
½ cup chopped fresh parsley
   (optional)
1 cup prepared GOOD
   SEASONS Italian Salad
   Dressing

PREPARE pasta as directed on
package; drain. Rinse with cold
water; drain.

MIX pasta, vegetables, olives,
cheese and parsley in large bowl.
Add dressing; toss to coat.

SERVE immediately or refrigerate
until ready to serve.
   Makes 8 servings

Prep Time: 25 minutes

Pasta Garden Salad

Cool Chicken Salad

- 2 cups STOVE TOP Chicken Flavor Stuffing Mix in the Canister
- ½ cup hot water
- 2 cups shredded lettuce
- 1½ cups chopped cooked chicken
- 1 small red pepper, chopped
- 2 tablespoons chopped fresh mint
- 2 tablespoons sliced green onion
- ¼ cup olive oil
- 2 tablespoons red wine vinegar

MIX stuffing mix and hot water in large bowl just to moisten. Let stand 5 minutes. Stir in lettuce, chicken, pepper, mint and onions.

MIX oil and vinegar in small bowl. Add to stuffing mixture; toss lightly. Serve immediately.

Makes 4 servings

Prep Time: 20 minutes

Chef's Stuffing Salad

- 2 cups STOVE TOP Chicken Flavor Stuffing Mix in the Canister
- ½ cup hot water
- 1 cup cherry tomatoes, cut into wedges
- 4 ounces cooked turkey, cut into thin strips
- 2 ounces Swiss cheese, cut into thin strips
- 2 ounces ham, cut into thin strips
- ⅓ cup red onion strips
- ½ cup prepared GOOD SEASONS Italian Salad Dressing

MIX stuffing mix and hot water in large bowl just to moisten. Let stand 5 minutes.

STIR in tomatoes, turkey, cheese, ham and onion. Add dressing; toss lightly. Serve immediately.

Makes 4 servings

Prep Time: 15 minutes

Treat your green salads to a sprinkle of STOVE TOP Stuffing Mix in the Canister instead of croutons. Or, add excitement to vegetables with a sprinkle of stuffing mix just before serving.

Top to bottom: Cool Chicken Salad, Chef's Stuffing Salad

Picante Beans and Rice

1 can (16 ounces) kidney
    beans, undrained
1 cup water
¾ cup picante sauce or salsa
1½ cups MINUTE Original Rice,
    uncooked
    Chopped cilantro or fresh
    parsley (optional)

BRING beans, water and picante
sauce to boil in medium saucepan.

STIR in rice; cover. Remove from
heat. Let stand 5 minutes. Stir.
Sprinkle with cilantro.

Makes 6 servings

Prep Time: 5 minutes
Cooking Time: 10 minutes

Rice 'n Cheese

1 cup milk
½ cup water
2 teaspoons margarine or
    butter
¼ teaspoon salt
6 slices (⅔ or ¾ ounce *each*)
    American cheese
1½ cups MINUTE Original Rice,
    uncooked

BRING milk, water, margarine and
salt to boil in medium saucepan.
Add cheese; stir until completely
melted. Return to boil.

STIR in rice; cover. Remove from
heat. Let stand 5 minutes. Stir.

Makes 4 servings

Prep Time: 5 minutes
Cooking Time: 10 minutes

Picante Beans and Rice

Nicoise-Style Tuna Salad

1 cup fresh green beans, halved
1 can (12½ ounces) tuna packed in water, drained, broken into chunks
½ cup quartered cherry tomatoes
¼ cup diagonally sliced celery
¼ cup pitted ripe olives, halved
¼ cup chopped green onions
2 tablespoons chopped fresh parsley
½ cup prepared GOOD SEASONS Fat Free Italian Salad Dressing
Salad greens
1 hard-cooked egg, quartered

COOK beans in enough boiling water to cover in medium saucepan 4 minutes or until tender-crisp. Drain. Rinse with cold water; drain.

MIX beans, tuna, tomatoes, celery, olives, onions and parsley in large bowl. Add dressing; toss to coat well.

SERVE on salad greens. Garnish with egg.

Makes 3 to 4 servings

Prep Time: 20 minutes

Chicken Berry Salad

1 envelope GOOD SEASONS Honey Mustard Salad Dressing Mix
Orange juice
8 cups torn mixed salad greens
1 pound cooked chicken, cut into strips
2 cups assorted berries (blueberries, raspberries, sliced strawberries)
1 package (8 ounces) frozen sugar snap peas, thawed
½ cup toasted pecans *or* slivered almonds

PREPARE salad dressing mix as directed on envelope, substituting orange juice for water.

MIX greens, chicken, berries, snap peas and pecans in large bowl. Add dressing; toss lightly. Serve immediately.

Makes 4 to 6 servings

Prep Time: 20 minutes

In search of an easy side dish elegant enough for company? Dress up hot cooked carrots, baked acorn, hubbard or butternut squash or sweet potatoes with a little LOG CABIN Syrup and a touch of ground ginger or cinnamon. Or, try LOG CABIN Syrup with cooked pearl onions, plus a little orange peel and dried thyme leaves.

Sweet Surprises

*O*ur collection of
*homemade favorites
includes some American
classics. Who can resist
dessert when it's Chocolate
Dip Delight, Mapley Berry
Shortcake or the Southern
classic Bananas Foster? Rice
pudding lovers will enjoy
Vanilla Rice Pudding
with its three delicious
variations. In addition,
there are even more sweet
snacks as memorable as
Mom's, but now a lot
easier to make.*

*With a few ingredients right
from your shelf, you can
enjoy the old-fashioned
goodness of homemade
treats any night of the week.
Because we've minimized
the preparation steps, these
recipes are now easy to
make, and require little
cleanup.*

Mapley Berry Shortcake

1 cup blueberries
1 cup sliced strawberries
½ cup LOG CABIN Syrup,
  divided
1 cup whipping (heavy) cream
4 sponge cake dessert shells

MIX berries and 3 tablespoons of
the syrup in small bowl. Let stand
15 minutes.

BEAT cream and ¼ cup of the
syrup in medium bowl with
electric mixer on medium speed
until soft peaks form.

BRUSH dessert shells lightly with
remaining 1 tablespoon syrup. Top
with berry mixture and whipped
cream. Serve immediately. Store
leftover dessert in refrigerator.
                    Makes 4 servings

Prep Time: 30 minutes

Mapley Berry Shortcake

Chocolate Dip Delight

Chocolate Dip Delight

⅔ cup whipping (heavy) cream
½ cup LOG CABIN Syrup
1 package (8 ounces) BAKER'S
   Semi-Sweet Chocolate
   Assorted fresh or dried fruit,
   cake cubes, cookies or
   pretzels

BRING cream and syrup to boil in small saucepan on medium heat, stirring constantly. Remove from heat. Stir in chocolate until melted. Serve warm as a dip with fruit, cake cubes, cookies or pretzels.

Makes about 1¾ cups

Prep Time: 5 minutes
Cooking Time: 5 minutes

Maple-Flavored Bread Pudding

¾ cup milk
¾ cup LOG CABIN Syrup
3 eggs
¼ teaspoon ground nutmeg
    (optional)
    Dash salt
4 slices white bread, toasted,
    cut into 1-inch pieces
    (about 2½ cups)
½ cup chopped nuts

HEAT oven to 400°F.

BRING milk and syrup just to boil in small saucepan on medium heat, stirring occasionally. Remove from heat.

BEAT eggs, nutmeg and salt in large bowl with wire whisk or fork until well blended. Gradually beat in hot milk mixture. Stir in bread and nuts. Pour into greased 2-quart casserole.

BAKE 20 minutes or until pudding is set. Serve warm.
                    Makes 4 to 6 servings

Prep Time: 10 minutes
Cooking Time: 20 minutes

Try this in-a-minute mapley topping: Beat together 1 cup whipping (heavy) cream with ¼ cup LOG CABIN Syrup until soft peaks form.

Bananas Foster

6 tablespoons margarine or
    butter
½ cup LOG CABIN Syrup
2 tablespoons chopped pecans
1 tablespoon lemon juice
½ teaspoon ground cinnamon
3 bananas, split, halved
    Vanilla ice cream

MELT margarine in large skillet on medium heat. Stir in syrup, pecans, lemon juice and cinnamon. Bring to boil. Reduce heat to low; simmer 3 minutes or until blended and slightly thickened.

STIR in bananas. Simmer 3 minutes, basting occasionally with syrup mixture. Serve over ice cream.   *Makes 4 servings*

Prep Time: 5 minutes
Cooking Time: 10 minutes

A great cleanup tip: When measuring LOG CABIN Syrup for recipe use, spray measuring cup with no stick spray coating before filling with syrup.

Creamy Fruit Drizzle

2 cups sour cream
1 envelope GOOD SEASONS
    Honey Mustard Salad
    Dressing Mix
2 tablespoons brown sugar
1 tablespoon grated lemon
    peel

MIX sour cream, salad dressing mix, sugar and lemon peel in medium bowl until well blended.

DRIZZLE over fresh fruit or use as topping or dip. Store leftover dressing mixture in refrigerator.

Makes 2 cups

Prep Time: 5 minutes

Nutty Dessert Sauce

1 cup LOG CABIN Syrup
⅓ cup margarine or butter
1 cup toasted chopped walnuts

COOK syrup and margarine in medium saucepan on low heat until margarine is melted, stirring occasionally. Remove from heat. Stir in walnuts. Cool 10 minutes or until slightly thickened. Serve over ice cream or pound cake.

Makes about 1⅔ cups

Prep Time: 5 minutes
Cooking Time: 10 minutes

Touch of Maple Frosting

1 package (3 ounces)
    PHILADELPHIA BRAND
    Cream Cheese, softened
3 tablespoons margarine or
    butter, softened
2 tablespoons LOG CABIN
    Syrup
2 cups powdered sugar

BEAT cream cheese, margarine and syrup in medium bowl with electric mixer on low speed until well blended. Gradually beat in sugar until well blended and smooth.

*Makes 1½ cups or enough to
cover top of 13×9-inch cake or
frost 18 cupcakes*

Prep Time: 10 minutes

---

*Sweeten up a summer afternoon
with a refreshing cooler: Add
LOG CABIN Syrup to iced coffee or
your favorite milk shake.*

Creamy Fruit Drizzle

Top to bottom: Mapley Butter Spread, Oat Muffins

Oat Muffins

1½ cups flour
2 teaspoons CALUMET Baking Powder
¼ teaspoon salt
2 eggs
2 tablespoons brown sugar
¾ cup milk
½ cup LOG CABIN Syrup
¼ cup oil
1 cup quick-cooking oats
½ cup chopped walnuts

HEAT oven to 400°F.

MIX flour, baking powder and salt in large bowl. Beat eggs, sugar, milk, syrup and oil in small bowl. Add to flour mixture; stir just until moistened. (Batter will be lumpy.) Gently stir in oats and walnuts. Spoon batter into greased or paper-lined muffin pan, filling each cup ⅔ full.

BAKE 20 minutes or until golden brown. *Makes 1 dozen*

Prep Time: 10 minutes
Cooking Time: 20 minutes

Mapley Butter Spread

½ cup (1 stick) butter or margarine, softened
¼ cup LOG CABIN Syrup
2 tablespoons raisins (optional)

BEAT butter in small bowl until smooth. Add syrup; beat until light and fluffy. Stir in raisins.

SPREAD on muffins or toast, if desired. Store leftover spread in refrigerator.

Makes about ¾ cup

Prep Time: 5 minutes

Granola Snack

1 cup quick-cooking oats
⅔ cup BAKER'S ANGEL FLAKE
   Coconut
¼ cup chopped pitted prunes
¼ cup chopped dried apricots
¼ cup raisins
2 tablespoons sunflower seed
2 tablespoons sesame seed
2 tablespoons brown sugar
¼ cup oil
¼ cup LOG CABIN Syrup

HEAT oven to 325°F.

MIX oats, coconut, prunes, apricots, raisins, sunflower seed, sesame seed and sugar in large bowl.

BRING oil and syrup to boil in small saucepan on medium heat, stirring constantly. Pour over oat mixture. Mix to coat well. Spread evenly in 13×9-inch baking pan.

BAKE 20 minutes, stirring several times to toast evenly. Press mixture into 1-inch-thick layer on tray, using back of spoon. Cool. Break into bite-size pieces. Store in tightly covered container.

Makes about 5 cups

Prep Time: 10 minutes
Cooking Time: 20 minutes

Peanut Butter Bars

⅔ cup sugar
⅔ cup LOG CABIN Syrup
1½ cups chunky peanut butter
3 cups corn flakes
4 squares BAKER'S Semi-Sweet
   Chocolate, melted

BRING sugar and syrup to boil in medium saucepan on medium heat, stirring occasionally. Remove from heat. Stir in peanut butter.

POUR syrup mixture over cereal in large bowl. Mix to coat well. Spread in greased 13×9-inch pan. Spread with melted chocolate. Let stand until chocolate is firm. Cut into bars.

Makes about 3 dozen

Prep Time: 25 minutes

Need a quick dessert? Serve canned pears or peaches with a swirl of LOG CABIN Syrup. Or, try syrup over ice cream or yogurt.

Mapley Fruit Dip

1 container (8 ounces) sour cream
⅓ cup LOG CABIN Syrup
¼ teaspoon ground cinnamon
⅛ teaspoon ground nutmeg
Assorted fresh fruit, cake cubes *or* cookies

MIX sour cream, syrup, cinnamon and nutmeg in small bowl.

SERVE as dip with fruit, cake cubes or cookies. Store leftover dip in refrigerator.

Makes about 1⅓ cups

Prep Time: 5 minutes

Easy Cream Cheese Spread

1 container (8 ounces) PHILADELPHIA BRAND Soft Cream Cheese
¼ cup LOG CABIN Syrup

MIX cream cheese and syrup in small bowl until smooth.

SPREAD on muffins or bagels, if desired. Store leftover spread in refrigerator.

Makes about 1 cup

Prep Time: 5 minutes

Mapley Fruit Dip

Mapley Pecan Muffins

Mapley Pecan Muffins

2 cups flour
¼ cup firmly packed brown sugar
1½ teaspoons CALUMET Baking Powder
¼ teaspoon salt
1 egg
½ cup milk
½ cup LOG CABIN Syrup
⅓ cup margarine or butter, melted
1 teaspoon vanilla
1 cup chopped pecans
1 tablespoon granulated sugar
⅛ teaspoon ground cinnamon

HEAT oven to 400°F.

MIX flour, brown sugar, baking powder and salt in large bowl. Beat egg in small bowl; stir in milk, syrup, margarine and vanilla. Add to flour mixture; stir just until moistened. (Batter will be lumpy.) Stir in pecans. Spoon batter into greased or paper-lined muffin pan, filling each cup ⅔ full.

MIX granulated sugar and cinnamon in small bowl. Sprinkle over batter.

BAKE 20 minutes or until golden brown.   *Makes 1 dozen*

Prep Time: 10 minutes
Cooking Time: 20 minutes

Vanilla Rice Pudding

- **4 cups milk**
- **1 egg, well beaten**
- **1 package (4-serving size) JELL-O Vanilla Flavor Cook and Serve Pudding and Pie Filling**
- **1 cup MINUTE Original Rice, uncooked**
- **¼ cup raisins (optional)**
- **Ground cinnamon (optional)**
- **Ground nutmeg (optional)**

GRADUALLY stir milk and egg into pudding mix in large saucepan. Stir in rice and raisins. Cook and stir on medium heat until mixture just comes to boil. Cool 5 minutes, stirring twice.

POUR into individual dessert dishes or serving bowl. Serve warm or refrigerate, if desired. (Place plastic wrap on surface of pudding while cooling.) Sprinkle with cinnamon and nutmeg just before serving.   *Makes 10 servings*

Prep Time: 5 minutes
Cooking Time: 20 minutes

Double Chocolate Rice Pudding: Prepare as directed above, using chocolate flavor pudding mix. Stir in 2 squares BAKER'S Semi-Sweet Chocolate, chopped, with rice. Omit raisins, cinnamon and nutmeg.

Applesauce Rice Pudding: Prepare as directed above, using 3 cups milk. Stir in 1½ cups chunky applesauce and ½ teaspoon ground cinnamon with rice. Omit raisins and nutmeg.

Pumpkin Rice Pudding: Prepare as directed above, using 3 cups milk. Stir in 1 can (16 ounces) pumpkin, ⅓ cup firmly packed brown sugar, ½ teaspoon ground cinnamon and ¼ teaspoon ground ginger with rice. Omit raisins and nutmeg.

Vanilla Rice Pudding

Index

METRIC CONVERSION CHART

VOLUME MEASUREMENTS (dry)

⅛ teaspoon = 0.5 mL
¼ teaspoon = 1 mL
½ teaspoon = 2 mL
¾ teaspoon = 4 mL
1 teaspoon = 5 mL
1 tablespoon = 15 mL
2 tablespoons = 30 mL
¼ cup = 60 mL
⅓ cup = 75 mL
½ cup = 125 mL
⅔ cup = 150 mL
¼ cup = 175 mL
1 cup = 250 mL
2 cups = 1 pint = 500 mL
3 cups = 750 mL
4 cups = 1 quart = 1 L

VOLUME MEASUREMENTS (fluid)

1 fluid ounce (2 tablespoons) = 30 mL
4 fluid ounces (½ cup) = 125 mL
8 fluid ounces (1 cup) = 250 mL
12 fluid ounces (1½ cups) = 375 mL
16 fluid ounces (2 cups) = 500 mL

WEIGHTS (mass)

½ ounce = 15 g
1 ounce = 30 g
3 ounces = 90 g
4 ounces = 120 g
8 ounces = 225 g
10 ounces = 285 g
12 ounces = 360 g
16 ounces = 1 pound = 450 g

DIMENSIONS

1/16 inch = 2 mm
⅛ inch = 3 mm
¼ inch = 6 mm
½ inch = 1.5 cm
¾ inch = 2 cm
1 inch = 2.5 cm

OVEN TEMPERATURES

250°F = 120°C
275°F = 140°C
300°F = 150°C
325°F = 160°C
350°F = 180°C
375°F = 190°C
400°F = 200°C
425°F = 220°C
450°F = 230°C

BAKING PAN SIZES

Utensil	Size in Inches/ Quarts	Metric Volume	Size in Centimeters
Baking or Cake Pan (square or rectangular)	8×8×2	2 L	20×20×5
	9×9×2	2.5 L	22×22×5
	12×8×2	3 L	30×20×5
	13×9×2	3.5 L	33×23×5
Loaf Pan	8×4×3	1.5 L	20×10×7
	9×5×3	2 L	23×13×7
Round Layer Cake Pan	8×1½	1.2 L	20×4
	9×1½	1.5 L	23×4
Pie Plate	8×1¼	750 mL	20×3
	9×1¼	1 L	23×3
Baking Dish or Casserole	1 quart	1 L	—
	1½ quart	1.5 L	—
	2 quart	2 L	—